MICHAEL JA

Rick Sky is the p[...] *Mirror*, and has inter[...] world's top rock stars. He has contributed to dozens of publications all around the world, including *Spin*, *The Chicago Tribune* and *Max*, and is the author of *The Show Must Go On: The Life of Freddie Mercury* and *The Take That Fact File*.

RICK SKY

MICHAEL JACKSON

The Bad Year

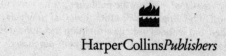

HarperCollins*Publishers*

HarperCollins*Publishers*
77–85 Fulham Palace Road,
Hammersmith, London W6 8JB

A Paperback Original 1994
1 3 5 7 9 8 6 4 2

A catalogue record for this book
is available from the British Library

ISBN 0 00 638373 4

Set in Linotron Meridien by
Rowland Phototypesetting Ltd
Bury St Edmunds, Suffolk

Printed in Great Britain by
HarperCollinsManufacturing Glasgow

CONTENTS

For my family

CHAPTER 1

The Start of the Troubles

IT WAS AN ODD PLACE for Michael Jackson to start a tour –
Bangkok, the sex capital of the world – a place where easy
sex was rife, a place where all kinds of sex, even sex with
young children, could be bought for just a fistful of dollars.

That Michael Jackson should be in Bangkok when the
news first erupted was pure irony. The star was seen as the
high priest of asexuality, a paragon of sexual innocence;
he was the man who had admitted to being a virgin and
he was about to become embroiled in the biggest sex scandal the entertainment world had ever seen. The news hit
with all the force of a Californian earthquake and was just
as devastating.

Reports from the singer's home state claimed that
Jackson was at the centre of child abuse allegations. To
most people it was tantamount to saying that Mother
Teresa was a murderess, Pope John Paul was the head of
the Mafia or that Princess Diana was a Madam in charge
of a high-class brothel; or, in an analogy better suited to
the childlike star who seemed to lead his life as if he were
the hero of a Disney cartoon, that Mickey Mouse was a
pornographer, Goofy a heroin dealer and Donald Duck a
serial killer. It was just unbelievable because, to the public
at large, Jackson was a thirty-five-year-old man-child who
was steadfastly religious, and whose favourite pastimes

were watching cartoons, larking about on funfair rides and playing computer games.

Moreover, Jackson adored children and had built his whole life around them. He was one of show business's most generous stars and had devoted much of his time and energy to children, giving away millions from his multimedia fortune to help poor and underprivileged youngsters all around the world.

This series of dates in the Far East, which formed the second leg of his *Dangerous* tour, started in the sweltering heat of August and was set to end just before Christmas 1993. It should have been one of the high spots of the star's glittering career and was set to rake in a staggering £40 million. He was about to play many places he had never previously toured, and he found that part of the world fascinating and exotic. He adored its charming and polite people and its colourful customs.

The people who had been bombarded with images of the child-loving superstar couldn't wait for him to arrive in the city. When tickets went on sale in July fans camped overnight in the meandering, bustling streets to make sure they got their hands on what was deemed the hottest ticket in town. As Jackson arrived in Bangkok children followed his every step. In fact the superstar was in the city to make money for children. At a special press conference his sponsors, the soft drinks giant Pepsi-Cola, handed over a $50,000 (£33,000) cheque for children's charities. Jackson was accompanied by a dozen garland-bearing youngsters.

But as the unbelievable allegations bounced across the globe, Jackson's triumphant arrival in Bangkok seemed like a distant dream. As he watched the early morning news in his splendid suite in the Oriental, one of the world's most luxurious hotels, he looked pale and drawn. The self-proclaimed king of pop had been welcomed as royalty in Bangkok, but now his crown felt uneasy on his head. The last few days had not been good ones for him: the heat in Bangkok was oppressive and was making him feel dehydrated; he was worried about how his new stage show would go down in the Far East; and then there was Evan Chandler.

Evan Chandler was the father of a thirteen-year-old boy, Jordan, and he claimed that Michael Jackson had abused his son. As a star, Jackson had of course been at the centre of all kinds of rumours and malicious gossip, and had been hounded by all sorts of crackpots. But this was something different. This was a claim that even the Los Angeles police were investigating, after being told of the alleged abuse by the young boy's therapist, Dr Mathis Abrams, who under Californian law was required to report any suspected abuse to the authorities.

As Jackson rehearsed for the all-important first show of the tour, a lieutenant from the Los Angeles Police Department was interviewing Jordan Chandler and taking a statement from him. On 21 August a search warrant was issued and the police raided Jackson's Neverland ranch in Santa Barbara and a secret apartment he had bought in the centre of Los Angeles. It was a thorough, lengthy and extensive raid. The police had even taken a locksmith to make sure that they could enter every room and explore the secret recesses of the ranch's innermost sanctuaries and private rooms. Accompanying them to the ranch were the Child Protective Services, the social services organization which is normally called in when a child is allegedly sexually or physically abused or exploited.

After a three-hour search the police took away a collection of photographs and documents. They were tight-lipped about the affair and remained so throughout the whole scandal, although when the news broke Commander David Gascon of the Los Angeles Police Department admitted:

We are approaching the investigation very carefully and very methodically. It is criminal, it is official and it will be professionally handled. On 17 August the Los Angeles Police Department initiated a criminal investigation of entertainer Michael Jackson. We have been in contact with the district attorney's office. We are not disclosing any aspect of the investigation at this point. We are taking this situation very seriously.

Another police officer added: 'Specific allegations have been made and searches have been carried out with regard to the contents and layout of Mr Jackson's house and apartment.'

When Jackson stepped on to the stage in front of the army of 20,000 screaming fans it was a brief respite from the scandal and from the problems that had been troubling his mind all day. For ninety minutes he was able to escape from all the pressure as he danced twinkle-toed around the stage, putting on a brilliant show – a show that had made him one of the legends in pop history. On stage he created pure magic as his parade of hits filled the sweltering air of the stadium. The stage was where Jackson really came alive; on the stage, he once confessed to me, he felt more at home than anywhere else. But as the cheers faded away after the final encore, he could no longer dispel the nightmare scenario that he had found himself in. It was a scenario that the sensitive superstar tried his best not to inflame. He was advised by his lawyers – among the battalion of aides he employed to keep his multi-million-pound fortune pumping out more and more money – to make a statement about the allegations that threatened his career.

The statement was brief and was issued through one of his lawyers, Howard Weitzman, a well-known celebrity lawyer. Weitzman had recently defended beautiful actress

Kim Basinger in the breach of contract action against her. A distraught Jackson told of his horror at the accusations and protested — albeit briefly — his innocence. It was a statement that pacified the millions of Jackson fans around the world who were worried sick about their star: 'I am horrified by the allegation. It is horrendous. I am confident that the Los Angeles police will conduct a fair and thorough investigation and that its result will demonstrate there is no wrong-doing on my part. I intend to continue with my world tour and look forward to seeing all of you soon. I am grateful for your overwhelming support.'

However, despite Jackson's determination to carry on with the tour as normal and not to disappoint the fans he adored so much, the stress and pressure of the scandal forced him to cancel the next day's show in Bangkok just three hours before he was meant to go on stage, leaving thousands of fans upset. As the superstar lay in bed, his doctor, Stuart Finkelstein, said that he was suffering from active dehydration caused by heat and humidity. The very high temperature in Bangkok, which was in the middle of the rainy season, had taken its toll on the sensitive star, who had done everything he could to try to appear on stage and give the performance of a lifetime, he said. 'I have started intravenous treatment for dehydration and Michael is improving. He expends so much effort and energy because his performance is so important to him.'

The show's promoter, Brian Marcer, said the pressure on Jackson was too great. 'Seventeen songs in this heat and humidity, it was just too much for him. He was taking oxygen backstage after every second song. The day before the show he didn't eat all day and he just couldn't get up. He decided to cancel the second show at 5 p.m.'

As Jackson lay in his hotel bedroom the scandal began to unfold in greater detail and the world's media hungrily gobbled up every detail.

*   *   *

The meeting that brought together Michael Jackson and the thirteen-year-old boy who almost ruined his career was pure accident. It took place in May 1992, just before Jackson launched his eagerly-awaited *Dangerous* tour, his first concert tour for four years. The star's car broke down and he found himself stranded. His aides phoned a car rental agency they regularly used for a replacement. The agency, Rent-a-Wreck, was one of Los Angeles' most hip and quirky organizations. Jackson, in common with many celebrities, liked using their cars because this meant he could remain anonymous. The store's owner, David Schwartz, told his wife to rush over straight away with a new car to where Jackson had stalled. The dark-haired, olive-skinned June, a beautiful ex-model, took along her daughter Lily and her son Jordan, then twelve years old.

Like kids all over the world, Jordan was a huge Michael Jackson fan, but never in his wildest dreams did he imagine that the superstar would become sweet on him. But immediately after their first meeting, Jackson began calling Jordan on a daily basis and their strange and intimate relationship began.

While he was on tour, Michael Jackson could not get the twelve-year-old boy with the soulful eyes and the mop of jet-black hair out of his mind. He began calling him regularly from various points along his route, which took in countries from Sweden to Romania. It was, say those who believe the allegations against Jackson, a warm courtship – although the more cynical claim it was the kind of friendship that Michael Jackson had with a number of boys. Jordan Chandler's gifted lawyer, Larry Feldman, told the American magazine *Vanity Fair*: 'Michael was in love with the boy. It was a gentle, soft, caring, warm, sweet relationship.'

The young boy was spellbound by the star. They talked about everything from video games and cartoons to the wonderful menagerie Jackson kept at his fabulous home,

Neverland. But it was not until February of the following year that Jordan was able to experience the magic of the fairytale place himself – the place Jackson had named after the bewitching kingdom in the children's classic *Peter Pan*, the story of a boy who never grew up.

When Jackson first invited Jordan and his family to stay with him at Neverland for the weekend they slept in the guest house, which is some way from the main house. More trips to Neverland followed and during one of these Jackson took Jordan and his half-sister on a special trip to the children's store Toys 'R' Us, where he lavished presents on them. These were the first of a cornucopia of gifts and delights that Jordan was to heap on the children and their forty-year-old mother. Jackson began to spend every weekend with his 'new family', which is what Jordan, June and Lily had effectively become. Jackson and Jordan became inseparable and indulged in all kinds of childish games from battling against each other in video games to having water pistol fights. They were having such fun.

In May Jackson even took Jordan, June and Lily with him to Monte Carlo for the World Music Awards, where he collected three prestigious trophies. Jordan sat on Jackson's lap throughout the ceremony, next to Prince Albert of Monaco. It was at the end of the evening, as stars including Michael Douglas, Patrick Swayze, Tina Turner and Rod Stewart left the event, that a crazy fan made a lunge at Jackson in full view of his 'family'. As Jackson fell to the ground and security men leapt to his aid, whisking him to safety, Lily cried out, 'Someone's hurting Michael. Don't let them.'

Jordan's mother originally thought that Jackson's friendship with her young boy was quite harmless. Indeed, she believed that Jackson was good for her son, as he had been good to so many other children, and that Jackson genuinely loved her son. She saw nothing sinister or selfish about his behaviour. All she knew was that when Jordan and Jackson were together the young boy seemed happier and more full of fun that he had ever been. Jordan's father, however, thought differently. When he saw Jackson and his son in bed together he was horrified. He was not as convinced as his ex-wife of the innocence of it all. They might have been fully clothed but he didn't like it. He thought it abnormal and unnatural and he decided to take steps to stop it . . . and unleashed a scandal which came close to ruining Michael Jackson's career.

At first Evan Chandler seemed happy that his son was friends with such an important celebrity. The wealthy dentist had dreams of being a major player on the Hollywood scene and knew that rubbing shoulders with a star like Michael Jackson could help him to make those dreams come true. He was already a bit player on the scene, having written the script for the Mel Brooks comedy, *Robin Hood: Men in Tights,* and he was eager for more. But his dreams of a showbiz career were tarnished with fears. His son's friendship with Michael Jackson began to prey on his mind more and more and the worry began to eat at him. One day it all got too much and he broke down in tears while he was treating one of his patients, a Beverly Hills lawyer called Barry Rothman.

When Rothman was told of Jordan's strange relationship with the singer he agreed to represent Chandler. One of the first things they decided to do was to demand a meeting with the dentist's ex-wife to discuss the young boy's future. By this time Chandler felt that he was being ousted from his son's life by the singer. He was worried that Jordan might even be forgetting all about his father. Jordan was not turning up to see him as much as he once used to on the days that had been set aside for visitation rights, and Chandler was worried sick that his family was being torn apart.

June thought that her ex-husband was desperately

over-reacting to the situation and she turned to the one person she had become close to over the last few months – Michael Jackson – and confided to him everything that was going on.

Jackson was stunned by what was happening, and was frightened of losing the boy and the new family he had made for himself, which aides said had made him blissfully happy. He called in his own lawyer, Bertram Fields, to try to get the matter sorted out. To many it might have seemed strange that a lawyer such as Fields, whose usual rate for sorting out show-business matters is £350 per hour, should get involved in what appeared to be a humdrum custody battle, but Jackson was adamant that Fields help him out. Fields, who has handled the affairs of numerous top celebrities, decided to call in one of the country's top private eyes, Anthony Pellicano – a tough-talking ex-cop from Chicago who had made his name in Hollywood circles with his no-nonsense approach and had worked with Jackson as his security adviser over the last four years.

Jordan Chandler's lawyer, Larry Feldman, referred in an interview with *Vanity Fair* to the incongruity of having such big guns involved in what seemed then to be a minor family squabble: 'If this is such an innocent relationship, why have the likes of Fields and Pellicano involved?' he asked.

Around mid-July Jordan was given over to his father for one week's visitation. It was a crucial week: the young boy broke down in tears and allegedly confessed to his father that Michael Jackson had molested him. Boiling with anger and emotion, Evan Chandler refused to give his son back after the week was over, saying that Jordan had been brainwashed and seduced.

The next day June Schwartz signed an agreement saying that she would not take her son out of the county of Los Angeles without her ex-husband's consent. That, however, was not enough for Evan, who threatened to tell the world about the 'real' Michael Jackson and dispel the glossy image. He was ready to reveal the truth about the singer's personal life-style and his friendships with young boys.

Jordan's father insisted upon a meeting with the singer to try and thrash things out. This eventually took place on 4 August. It was at that meeting, which was also attended by his son and by Jackson's private detective, Pellicano, that Chandler was said to have read the singer a section of the criminal code about reporting child abuse in what seemed like a tactic to scare Jackson away from his son and to force him into a confession.

Pellicano claims that when that meeting began Evan Chandler was incredibly friendly with Michael, hugging him and kissing him. To him it seemed either that the father was just using Jackson or that he believed, as Jordan's mother did at the time, that Jackson was good to his boy. Pellicano said that he was astonished by the father's behaviour and told *Vanity Fair*: 'If I believed somebody molested my kid and I got that close to him, I'd be on death row right now.' But then things turned nasty, Pellicano claimed: the father accused Jackson of molesting his son and demanded that he set him up as a screenwriter.

Pellicano denied that there had been any offer of help in doing screenplays and the father got very angry. The meeting allegedly bust up at this point, with Chandler yelling at the terrified singer: 'You're going to be sorry, Michael. If I don't get what I want, Michael, I'm going to the press. I'm going to ruin you. I'm going to take you down.'

Later that day another meeting took place, this time between Pellicano and Evan Chandler's lawyer Barry Rothman. During that meeting Pellicano was told that Chandler wanted a $20-million (£13-million) trust fund set up for his son. Jackson's side saw this as a straightforward blackmail attempt, while those in the Chandler camp believe this was one of the options Evan Chandler had to stop Jackson in his tracks.

According to Pellicano, the deal involved Jackson setting up Dr Chandler as a Hollywood screenwriter with a $5-million (£3.25-million) 'salary' for four years. The money was to be paid in the form of four film projects. Later Pellicano said it was no more than a blackmail set-up: unless the demand was met the boy's father and lawyer threatened to accuse the singer of child molestation. Pellicano said he rejected this deal. However, police investigating these claims of blackmail found no evidence of a plot to extort money.

A few days later a second meeting took place between Pellicano and Rothman, this time with Evan Chandler also present. At this meeting Pellicano offered Chandler $350,000 (£230,000) as a 'film development deal', but claimed that the offer, which many later saw as hush money, did not suggest or imply that the sex abuse allegations against Jackson were true. Pellicano later said that the offer was made because he wanted to trap Chandler and show that he was involved in a blackmail racket: 'I was trying to set him up with the extortion. I wanted to see if he would take it. We had no intention of paying it. But I wanted them to accept it, they would have a contract and the whole thing would be over. I would get them out of my life and that would be it.'

Fields added: 'Pellicano was convinced that they would go for some kind of offer, some kind of cheque, and we'd have them.'

Nevertheless, whatever Pellicano's intentions, Chandler was not interested and refused the offer point blank.

The scene was now set for an almighty, vicious battle between all the lawyers involved, a battle which was to involve an avalanche of mud-slinging, leaked information and misinformation, and hostile smear campaigns.

As the two warring factions of lawyers battled it out against each other it became clear that the defence from Jackson's camp was basically that no sexual abuse had occurred and that Evan Chandler had coached his son into making up the stories about the singer who had befriended him in order to extort money from him.

Fields believes that the father invented the whole story of sexual abuse and molestation, told his son that this was their big chance to take Jackson to the cleaners and then even painstakingly told the boy exactly what to say. To support their claim that Chandler had coldly and calculatingly planned a detailed blackmail operation Jackson's camp even claimed that Chandler got an unsuspecting Jackson to spend time at his house so that he could bug the room that Jordan shared with Jackson. Fields told *Vanity Fair*: 'I don't believe them. It could have happened in many ways. It could have been the father coaching the boy, supplemented by the police questioning – it could have been a combination of both.'

Fields also says that it was the lure of the money to be made out of Jackson that made the mother and the stepfather, David Schwartz, change their attitude to Jackson. When Evan Chandler first made his allegations they took Jackson's side; later they supported Jordan's father.

Pellicano claimed that Jordan's attitude towards Jackson had also changed. He said that, in an earlier meeting, Jordan was very shaken by the way his father was behaving towards Jackson. The young boy had no idea that the father, who had once been extremely friendly to the singer, was trying to trap him. Pellicano was making it clear that Jordan had been close to Jackson and loved him as a friend; he was stunned by what his father was doing. It was wily Pellicano's way of trying to turn the tables on Chandler.

Pellicano even claimed that Jordan had at one time totally refuted the sex allegations he had made against Jackson: when he questioned Jordan in detail one day in Michael Jackson's luxury Los Angeles apartment, he alleged the young boy told him that the singer had never masturbated him or touched him and that he had never even seen Jackson in the nude; and Jordan had reiterated what he had said to Pellicano when the detective brought Jackson into the room.

Pellicano also claimed that during the questioning Jordan had told him that his father 'just wants money', and that during one meeting his father had asked Jackson to build him a whole new home.

However, despite the fact that Pellicano was well known for being a surveillance wizard, none of these conversations was ever recorded. It seemed an incredible omission, though Pellicano did not see it that way: 'I did it on a whim. I had no idea what he was going to tell me.'

Nor did Pellicano tape the meeting where Chandler said he would ruin Jackson this time. He said that he didn't want to tape a conversation with his client on it. Yet other conversations which amounted to nothing *were* recorded, in an attempt to set people up and force them to admit they were blackmailing Jackson. During some of these conversations Pellicano tried in vain to get the opposing lawyers to start talking about the $20 million which he claimed Evan Chandler was demanding; he could not get them to talk about it during his taped calls.

Larry Feldman, Jordan's lawyer, denounced the claims that Evan Chandler was a blackmailer as a totally ludicrous fiction. According to him, it was Pellicano and not Evan Chandler who introduced the idea of paying for the screenplay: Pellicano thought it would be a way to get the relationship between the boy and his father on an even keel again. Evan Chandler's new lawyer, Richard Hirsch, added: 'We vehemently deny there is any distortion. The other side is raising the red herring of extortion which is not a defence to child molestation.'

But then the affair took a whole new turn which panicked Evan Chandler and forced his hand. June Schwartz's lawyer, Michael Freeman, informed her ex-husband's lawyer that he would be filing papers the next day that would compel the father to turn over his son to June by that evening.

Chandler, worried sick that he could now lose his son, knew that he had to act quickly. He took a drastic step to stop his son's friendship with Michael Jackson. He filed papers which sought to ban the superstar from seeing his son. These papers were lodged in the California Superior Court, as part of the battle between Chandler and his ex-wife to get custody of Jordan. They demanded that all contact between the young boy and the world's biggest pop star should cease immediately.

Those court papers, in which Chandler is referred to as the petitioner, June Schwartz as the respondent, and Jordan as the 'minor child', stated:

Respondent's right and visitation is subject to and expressly conditioned upon the following terms and conditions. Respondent shall not allow the minor child to have any contact or communication in any form, directly or indirectly, including, but not limited to, telephone communication with a third party adult male known as Michael Jackson.

In the event it is discovered respondent has violated this condition of reasonable visitation, she hereby agrees any subsequent visitation with the minor child shall be limited to situations in which a third person monitor approved by petitioner or approved by the court is present.

Then, on 17 August, Evan Chandler took Jordan to therapist Mathis Abrams, and suddenly all the private threats, deals, negotiations and counter-negotiations evaporated. Dr Abrams reported the child abuse allegations to the police, and a few days later the biggest scandal the pop world had ever seen broke out like a plague on the front pages of almost every newspaper in the world.

CHAPTER 2

Allegations and Denials

During that week in July Jordan told his father how he had spent weekends at Jackson's Neverland ranch. In a tearful confession, he revealed how the singer had showered him with sackfuls of presents, worth thousands of pounds – the kind of lavish gifts that only someone as rich as Jackson could spend on a boy he had met only a few months before. He also claimed that Jackson had sexually abused him.

The boy's emotional tale of his relationship with Michael Jackson gradually unfolded: on 28 March Michael Jackson had taken Jordan, June and Lily to Las Vegas on a sumptuous five-day holiday. A private jet whisked them from Santa Monica's airport to the gambling capital of the world, where they were installed in the Michael Jackson suite at the Mirage Hotel – owned by the star's friend, Steve Wynn. It was in that suite that Michael Jackson spent his first night in bed with Jordan.

It came about, as Jordan admitted during his emotional confessions to his father and, later, to his psychiatrist, because they had watched a horror video. The video, *The Exorcist*, a chilling Hollywood blockbuster about a youngster possessed by the devil, had frightened him out of his wits. To calm his nerves Jackson suggested that the two of them spend the night together in the singer's bed while

Jordan's mother and half-sister stayed in another bedroom in the suite.

As these tales tumbled out it seemed as if this friendship had begun with boyish play and then escalated into something much more serious. It was in Monte Carlo, Jordan Chandler claimed, that the sexual touching first became excessive and unwelcome. Jackson had taken Jordan, June and Lily to that tax haven which slumbers peacefully but expensively between France and Italy in May 1993 where they watched him receive a string of prizes at the World Music Awards. The innocent kissing had turned into more sensual kissing, which had led to fondling and then on to masturbation and oral sex, Jordan claimed. It was in Monte Carlo that Jackson allegedly masturbated Jordan, lovingly told him that their relationship was meant to be, and then told him not to breathe a word of what had happened to anyone.

These graphic claims so perturbed Evan Chandler that, early one morning, he rushed his son off to see Los Angeles psychiatrist, Dr Mathis Abrams, and at the same time started the custody battle to give him the right to look after his son and to stop him being cared for by his ex-wife, whom he blamed for allowing Jackson to become so intimate with the boy.

A month previously, Abrams had been told, via Chandler's lawyer, of a 'hypothetical' situation involving an intense friendship between a star and a young boy who were separated by an age-gap of twenty years. Evan wanted to know what he made of it. Abrams was also told that the father of the boy had seen the pair in bed on a number of occasions. He had absolutely no idea either that Chandler's son Jordan was involved or that Jackson was the alleged abuser.

In the report the Beverly Hills psychiatrist wrote after hearing about this hypothetical child abuse situation he stated:

The male child has had for several months an intensely emotional personal relationship with an idolized male who is more than twenty years his senior. A celebrity of some sort. The child spends much of his time in the company of this adult male and the relationship is described as inseparable. The child has on many occasions spent the night in the same bed as the adult male, although separate beds are available.

The child and the adult male have been observed in the same bed under the covers by both the child's mother and father on separate occasions. The father is greatly concerned about the psychological and physical impact of this and the nature of the relationship – and the message to the child by his mother's consenting attitude. Based on the above, the child appears to be at risk.

It was a damning report. But worse was to come. Evan himself came to see Abrams. This time there were no hypotheses, suppositions or make-believe anecdotes. The young boy involved with the famous celebrity was his own son Jordan and the celebrity none other than Michael Jackson. During a session which lasted for nearly three hours, Jordan told Abrams all about the relationship, including his allegations that Jackson had sexually abused him.

Dr Abrams filed another report after extensive counselling sessions with both Jordan and his father – a report in which the sexual allegations were spelled out in graphic detail by the young boy. Once those allegations had been made, the psychiatrist could not keep them to himself, for according to Californian law any claim of sexual abuse must be reported to the police and the appropriate authorities – in this case, welfare officers Sergeant Felix and Deputy Patricia Clemmons, who interviewed Jordan soon after his meeting with Abrams.

In the police report that followed the handing-over of
the statement Jordan had made to his psychiatrist, the
young boy again claimed that Jackson had fondled his
genitals and had oral sex with him. The statement said
that the sexual abuse had started in February and had
continued for five months: 'The perpetrator Michael Jackson has sexually molested the reporting child in his home,
at the perpetrator's home as well as in other places. Starting in February and continuing to June the reporting child
was in the company of the perpetrator.'

Jordan Chandler had told Dr Abrams how, after he and
the superstar started sleeping in the same bed, their
relationship developed to the point where Jackson was
kissing him on the mouth and fondling his private parts.
Jackson also apparently began rubbing up against him.

The report – in which Chandler is referred to as 'the
minor', his father as 'Fa', and his mother as 'Mo' – says:

> Minor states Mr Jackson took him, his mo and half-
> sister to Las Vegas and they watched *The Exorcist*.
> Minor said he was afraid and ended up sleeping in
> the same bed with Mr Jackson. Mo saw this and
> allowed it to continue. At first Mr Jackson would
> 'cuddle' him and kiss him on the cheek. Minor did
> not feel uncomfortable with this. Mr Jackson then
> began to rub up against minor while sleeping in bed.

In the report, Jordan continued: 'Over time Mr Jackson
graduated to kissing me on the mouth . . . one time he
was kissing me and he put his tongue in my mouth and I
said: "Don't do that." . . . He (Mr Jackson) started crying
. . . I guess he tried to make me feel guilty.' Chandler also
said that Jackson had put his hand on his bottom and his
tongue in his ear.

The report went on: 'Minor said that he would sometimes feel Mr Jackson had an erection, as did minor some-

times. Jackson told him their being together was "in the cosmos" and "meant to be" ... Later the perpetrator would masturbate in front of the reporting child. The perpetrator would get him to co-operate by telling him other relatives and children did these things, so it was okay for him to do it as well.'

Jordan claimed things got out of hand in Monte Carlo. According to the report:

'Minor stated Mr Jackson told him masturbation was "a wonderful thing". Later while lying next to each other in bed Mr Jackson put his hand on minor's penis over his shorts saying, "This is going to be great." Then he put his hands under his shorts and masturbated minor until minor had orgasm at which point Mr Jackson asked, "Was that good?"'

Chandler also alleged that Jackson had oral sex with him, masturbated in front of him and ordered him not to tell a soul about what they were doing. The report continued: 'Minor stated, "He (Mr Jackson) had me suck on one of his nipples while he masturbated."'

After Monte Carlo, according to the anguished Jordan, 'I didn't want to see him any more. As time went on the sexual contact between us increased. Michael said to me: "It is okay and natural." But I knew something was wrong.' He also claimed that when he tried to end his relationship with Jackson, Jackson threatened him by saying he would end up in a juvenile detention centre if he ever revealed details about what had happened between them: 'they'd both be in trouble if he breathed a word of what happened'.

The statement also alleged that Jordan's mother June saw her son and Michael in bed together in Las Vegas. Evan Chandler believed she turned a blind eye to Jackson's friendship with her son so that she could continue to enjoy her 'glitzy life-style', along with all the gifts that Jackson had given to her as the head of what he called his 'new family'.'

Because of this latest twist of events, and because Jordan had reportedly told the authorities concerned that he wanted to stay with his father, he was allowed to remain with Evan. Jordan repeatedly said that he was scared that if he were returned to his mother she would allow Jackson to see him again. He too thought she had become completely bound up in Jackson's opulent life-style. There seems to be good reason for the boy's fears: it is true that after the first occasion that he and Jackson slept together June Schwartz objected and a row followed. During this row Michael Jackson broke down and cried, claim sources. He told June that the four of them were a family, that he loved them, and that they should trust him. He told her that there was nothing sexual in him sleeping with Jordan; it was something special. He ended his emotional speech with tears still in his eyes, saying Jordan could sleep anywhere he wanted to. It was such a heartfelt speech that June was convinced that all the star wanted to do was to be in her son's company, and, knowing Jackson's love for children, she saw nothing wrong in that.

And at first Jordan enjoyed being cuddled and loved by the superstar – a love that physically manifested itself by warm hand-holding and playful pecks on the cheek. So it was that June Schwartz was brought around and, for the next three months – with few exceptions – she let her thirteen-year-old son and the man twenty-one years his senior share the same bed.

Jackson was rattled by these accusations but said very little beyond the brief statement he made through his lawyer Weitzman. But if Jackson didn't do much talking, his lawyers and aides immediately went on the offensive. Their main defence that these damning and damaging allegations were part of a vicious blackmail attempt was, at the outset of the affair, a plausible defence in theory. Jackson was one of the richest stars in the world and as such had been hustled by blackmailers throughout his career. Only a few months previously he had admitted that at least thirty people a year had tried to get money from him through criminal means. Pellicano immediately claimed that the superstar was once again merely the victim of a failed multi-million-dollar extortion plot.

In the past, these demands had always been dealt with discreetly. But Jackson's legal team did not get off to a good start with their blackmail defence. At first Pellicano declared that a woman had tried to extort the money from Jackson and, though she was never named, by inference he could only have been referring to June Schwartz. According to Pellicano:

> This mother who made the complaint made repeated demands for money to keep quiet about the allegations. When we did not pay a phonecall was made to the Child and Family Services. This person waited until Michael was out of the country and made one final attempt to get the money. When they did not get it, they did what they did. To do this on the eve of Michael's world tour is despicable.

But Jackson's corner was forced to backtrack immediately on these allegations that June Schwartz was the woman who had attempted to extort £14 million from Jackson. Her lawyer Michael Freeman pointed out that she was unaware of her son's abuse claims at that time; the first she knew of them was when the police admitted they had launched an investigation into the singer. 'She was shocked by the claims. Obviously she had no idea that anything was going on of that nature.' Freeman also pointed out that she was a wealthy woman in her own right and had categorically denied ever asking for a single cent from Jackson.

As Jackson took to his sick bed in Bangkok, and as his

aides battled furiously to deny all allegations, there were more ominous noises from Los Angeles. TV reporter Diane Dimond, who was one of the first journalists to break the scandal, told how the official documents which had been handed to the Los Angeles police were full of the most painfully intimate sexual detail. She also revealed how Jackson had taken the boy shopping and told him: 'Pick any presents you want. I'll buy them for you.'

In addition to claiming that the allegations of sexual molestation were part of a failed blackmail attempt, Jackson's legal wizards decided to argue that there was nothing sexual in Jackson sleeping with a boy. They contended that this was perfectly innocent behaviour and, to prove their claim, they drafted in two young boys who were friends of Jackson's to appear on prime-time American TV and speak out in defence of Michael. The case was fast becoming a trial by television.

By bringing forward these two boys they hoped to show that the singer was no child molester but an asexual man-child who took great pleasure in the innocent company of children – a star who saw it as part of his mission on earth to make children happy. Thus it was that a beautiful dark-haired, doe-eyed eleven-year-old boy called Brett Barnes appeared on TV on 26 August to admit that he too had slept with the singer but also to deny that there was anything at all sexual in it. He said that Michael Jackson was more like a father to him than anything else.

'I was on one side of the bed and he was on the other and it was a big bed. Michael hugged and kissed me, but he did it just like you would kiss your own mother or hug your own friend. Michael is very nice – very, very nice and he cares a lot about kids. Just say you went to a toy shop and saw a toy you wanted, he'll buy that. And if he's wearing a piece of jewellery and you say, "Oh, that's nice," he'll give it to you.

He's a great friend to play with, to love. He's like
your best friend only big. He kisses? Yeah. Like you
kiss your mother ... It's like I've known him all
my life, and in a past life. He loves you like he is
your own father or brother or sister or mother. He
hugs and kisses and nothing more.'

Australian-born Brett first visited the Jackson ranch,
together with his family, in December 1991 when Jackson
got in touch with him after receiving a letter from Brett's
sister. Ironically, the boy was staying at Neverland with his
mother and sister when the Los Angeles police raided it.

The second boy, Wade Robson, was also Australian. He
too was wheeled on to testify to Jackson's innocence and
benevolence. Ten-year-old Robson, who had appeared in
Jackson's *Black or White* and *Heal the World* videos, and who
had met Jackson when he won a Michael Jackson competition in Brisbane, said: 'It was just a slumber party. We both
had pyjamas on. He sleeps on one side of the bed and I sleep
on the other, and it's a big bed. We just go to sleep.'

These were both emotional, innocent speeches and they
helped turn the tide of opinion back in Jackson's favour.
Many people who heard them were convinced that
Jackson just enjoyed being with children and that there
were no ulterior motives involved.

Jackson's defence team were delighted with their
strategy of getting little Brett and little Wade to tell how
they had gone to bed with the singer. Those hostile to
Jackson, however, thought that the star was shooting himself in the foot by pursuing this line of defence. They
argued that it proved that Jackson's bedtime sessions with
Jordan could not be dismissed as just an isolated incident;
they were part of an overall behaviour pattern. And they
raised the question of whether it was normal for a man in
his thirties to sleep with such young boys.

CHAPTER 3

The Magic of Michael Jackson

MICHAEL JACKSON IS THE BIGGEST POP STAR in the world. His music, myth and magic have touched more fans all over the globe than those of any other star. There is hardly a country in the world that hasn't been captivated by his singing and dancing. And it is not only his music that has fascinated the world, but his fantastical life, too. His career has made him one of the richest men in the world, and has spawned a billion-dollar empire, the largest and the most powerful the entertainment world has ever seen. Jackson's publishing company is a goldmine that never stops earning money. It not only includes his multi-million-selling songs but most of the Beatles' hit songs too, including 'Yesterday', 'All You Need Is Love' and 'She Loves You'. Among the only Beatles songs that Jackson does not own are those from the films *Help!* and *A Hard Day's Night*. In addition to the Beatles' hits, which he acquired in 1988 for £30 million, Jackson's 4,000-strong publishing catalogue includes songs by Elvis Presley, UB40 and Little Richard. His personal fortune is estimated at £200 million. Hooked to Michael Jackson's astounding career are such international giants as Jackson's recording company, the Japanese conglomerate, Sony, and the soft-drink giant, PepsiCo.

Michael Jackson's record contract is the most lucrative

any pop star has ever signed. In March 1991 he inked a deal which became known as the billion-dollar deal. This took place after Sony Music bought Jackson's record company, Epic. The singer received a signing-on fee of £2 million, and a staggering royalty rate – 25 per cent of each record sold – twice what most big stars got. It was a deal the like of which the pop world had never seen and it made other superstars – many of whom had been ecstatic to get a royalty rate as high as 12 per cent – green with envy.

Sponsors have courted Michael Jackson assiduously throughout his career, and for the last decade he had been signed up with Pepsi-Cola, in the biggest endorsement deal ever made – worth an estimated £10 million to the singer. In February 1993, just six months before the scandal broke, Jackson received £1 million for a twenty-minute appearance at half time during the final of the American superbowl football competition. Jackson's business empire was a licence to print money which had showed no signs of ever flagging. Everything he touched didn't just turn to gold, it turned to platinum.

Jackson's *Dangerous* tour was set to be one of the most profitable in pop history. It was estimated that the European leg alone would gross around £60 million, and by the time the whole world tour was over it would have raked in a staggering £300 million. Part of the profits of the tour, which kicked off in Germany in June 1992, were to be donated to the singer's Heal the World charity – though exactly what percentage would be given was never announced. The big chiefs at Pepsi who sponsored the tour kept resolutely quiet about the money aspect. They refused to say how much Jackson had given the foundation or how much he would donate from tour profits.

When Jackson went to Bangkok his plan was to take his music ever further afield. The second leg of the tour was to last until December of 1993. The singer was due to play to over two million people, bringing in around £40 million. It was seen as a way of making sure that Jackson kept his position as the best and most successful pop star in the world. He was obsessed with retaining his crown as the king of pop in the face of some bitter rivalry from a parade of other leading acts – which is why he wanted to take his *Dangerous* tour on to such far-flung places as Argentina, Peru, Indonesia and India: places which most pop stars had never toured before.

Before he set out on the tour, I was told he would be travelling with a party of 240 people, including musicians and crew organizers. Everywhere he went he would be shadowed by at least ten bodyguards. He would be given every creature comfort to make sure that the gruelling and ambitious trek was as easy for him as possible. A source told me at the time:

> Michael will be bringing along his own vegetarian cook and his own masseur. And he is having his own special brand of popcorn and mineral water flown to wherever he goes. Many of the hotel suites and the private homes he will stay in will be redecorated strictly to his specifications. The rooms have to be vacuumed spotlessly and have fresh flowers, ionizers and air-purifiers in them. Michael is paranoid about germs and dust in the atmosphere and wants to make sure that wherever he stays has a 'pure atmosphere'.

Before the tour kicked off, tour production boss Benny Collins told me how Jackson had worked night and day to make sure the tour would be a thriller:

> Michael is a real hard worker. We have been getting this tour together since February. Some days we haven't finished working till three in the morning. But Michael wants to get everything right. He is a

perfectionist. No matter how hard he makes other people work, he makes himself work twice as hard. The show will be spectacular. It will last a couple of hours and Michael will be playing hits right from his early days. Not every date is in place yet, but it will be the longest tour he's ever done.

The tour was to be the biggest in pop history; from start to finish it would last eighteen months. During that time, and in the run-up to the launch, I got to see a lot of Michael Jackson. Our first meeting took place in the middle of the Californian desert: Jackson was throwing a huge dinner party just yards away from where he had been shooting his *In the Closet* video with the beautiful British model, Naomi Campbell, and fifty miles outside the fashionable Californian holiday resort of Palm Springs. The party was staged in conjunction with top pop TV station, MTV. MTV had run a competition offering dinner with Michael Jackson as the prize, and they had received a staggering 4.1 million entries from all over the world. Thirty lucky winners realized the dream of a lifetime: they were Michael's and MTV's special guests that night at the party, which was attended by a hundred privileged guests. Demi Woo from Taiwan told me: 'I still can't believe it's true. I can't believe I've met Michael. He's my absolute hero.'

The £150,000 bash was one of the most spectacular parties the pop world had ever seen: it featured leopards, panthers, elephants, camels, near-naked girl samba dancers, magicians and fire-eaters. Michael, decked out in a black shirt with red epaulettes and black satin trousers, arrived at the party at 7 o'clock, just an hour after breaking off from his video-shooting. The normally reclusive pop star revealed a side of his personality that he had kept under wraps for years – that of a fun-loving extrovert. We saw once again what Jackson was like when he really let his hair down. At one point he even led a conga line up and down the length of the makeshift tent where the party was held. As the evening went on, his smile got larger and larger. At one point he even gave us a private preview of his dancing skills: he got up on the dance floor and showed why he is such a disco thriller. He boogied with guests, including some of the skimpily clad Brazilian dancers dressed in yellow bras and G-strings who had earlier entertained him. I danced alongside him but found it hard to keep up with his frantic steps.

The singer, then thirty-three years old, was having such fun that he spent a whole two hours at the party, even posing for group pictures with the winners. For much of the time he chatted, laughed and joked with Naomi Campbell, who sat by his side. He seemed more relaxed and at ease than he had for a long time. Also sitting at the table with Jackson was his video director, top fashion photographer Herb Ritts. The video, in which Jackson is featured with Naomi Campbell and four flamenco dancers, was shot in black and white and Ritts was thrilled with it. He told me: 'Michael was a dream to work with. He is very receptive of new ideas. We should have finished already but we've had some bad weather.'

But the bash nearly started off on a nasty note. As he arrived, the animal-loving Michael went to stroke a baby leopard which snapped at him viciously. However, the singer refused to be daunted: he joked with the animal's trainer, gathered up a couple of the children who were waiting outside to meet him, and made his way into the party, where he was greeted with screams and shrieks from the waiting guests. He was escorted to the top table, where he sat down to sign autographs and talk to awestruck fans.

He himself was awestruck as he watched the fire-eaters, the acrobats and the dancers who had been summoned to perform for the king of all performers. He was astounded when one of the troupe lay on a four-foot bed of nails while a pretty girl walked all over his back. At this point,

Jackson sat a little three-year-old girl on his knee so she could get a better view of some of the show. He was just as impressed with the magician, who came to his table and performed a variety of dazzling card tricks. 'I'd like to do some of those,' he told him.

During the party Jackson confessed: 'I'm having a wonderful time. Some of these acts are amazing. It's a real fun atmosphere.' When his minders and aides tried to get him to go, Jackson wouldn't budge. He told them: 'I want to see the next act, it's a guy who walks on broken glass and eats it.' The star sat rooted in his chair for the next fifteen minutes as he marvelled at the daredevil performance.

The food was every bit as good as the entertainment. It had been prepared by Jackson's special Sikh chef, who runs a catering company called Ashaka and cooks all Jackson's meals for him.

The singer admitted he was thrilled about touring again for the first time in four years: 'I'm really looking forward to performing again. I love being on stage. I can't wait to come to Britain. I had a great time when I was in London recently.'

Despite his enjoyment, the party left Jackson whacked. When one of the MTV winners, Margarietta Carreras from New Jersey, asked him to dance the smiling star told her: 'I'd love to, but please excuse me this time, I feel a little tired.' Then the singer told MTV bosses, 'Thanks for everything, it's been a thriller of an evening,' and disappeared into the desert night.

The European leg of the tour, which kicked off in Munich, was to take in thirty-nine dates in just 102 days. The singer made his speech outlining his hopes for the Heal the World Foundation. But underneath all the idealism and charity were serious commercial issues. The tour would not only make millions for Jackson, but bosses at Pepsi-Cola, who were involved in setting up the launch, hoped that Jackson's series of dates would dramatically increase sales of their soft drinks. The Pepsi people, in fact, spoke more at the launch than Jackson did. We were told how Pepsi's sponsorship of the Jackson tour was the largest sponsorship deal ever between an entertainer and a corporation. We were also blitzed with a video preview of a new Pepsi commercial called *Dreams* and informed that Pepsi-Cola International markets some of the world's most popular soft-drink brands in over 165 countries and territories – in 1991 Pepsi-Cola's sales were £1 billion in the US and it was volume leader in fifty-five other countries.

The President of Pepsi-Cola Europe, Fred Miles, promoted the tour with the words:

> The sheer energy and magic of Michael Jackson is synonymous with the image of Pepsi. The children were thrilled to see Michael and it was a real pleasure to see the excitement on their faces. Millions of people all over the world will soon share what they felt today. We are privileged to assist Michael in his work for the Heal the World Foundation and hope that companies throughout the world will extend their generosity to help our next generation.

But Jackson's tour was thrown into chaos a week before it even started. The perfectionist star changed a large chunk of the act – including songs and choreography – with just days to go. I was told he had been hit by a bout of nerves in his desperation to make the *Dangerous* tour his biggest and best yet. Guitarist Dave Williams, who has worked with the singer for the last fourteen years, admitted:

> I've never seen Michael so hyped up in all the years I've worked with him. All the musicians and crew were really shocked when just a week ago Michael

walked into rehearsals and told us to get rid of almost everything. He even changed the whole choreography for the shows. At one point I thought we'd never get the show on the road in time for the starting date. But we've worked frantically all around the clock and got everything together. The show we've got now will be dynamite.

When the first show kicked off in Munich I was there reporting for my newspaper, the *Daily Mirror*. Though I loved the show and found it exhilarating, I could not help but see much of it as a re-hash of old material. Though the music and the staging were as spectacular as you would expect from a Jackson show, I felt I had seen a lot of it before, and I was disappointed that he had not put in more fresh ideas. If, in my review of the show, I was hard on Jackson, it was only because he is one of the greatest pop stars of all time and I expected far more of him. When, for example, he kicked off his *Bad* tour in Tokyo, I was thrilled by the spectacle and gave it a glowing review. But this time I wrote:

Four years ago Jackson was king as he stormed the world with his *Bad* tour. But on Saturday night that wasn't the case. The problem was that Jackson just hasn't moved on. His looks may have changed dramatically but his songs and his show have stayed the same. So much of the concert was a re-run of that tour that I felt as if I was watching an action replay. The staging of songs like 'Thriller', 'Beat It' and 'She's Out of My Life' is virtually the same. For 'Beat It' he stands high on a hydraulic platform which moves over the crowd. For 'She's Out of My Life' he breaks down and fakes tears in exactly the same way he did four years ago. There is some new material for fans but the problem here is that Jackson's *Dangerous* album isn't as sensational as his earlier LPs. Although one of the songs on it, 'Black or White' – for which he made a wondrous, if horribly confused video – was performed magnificently live and was one of the highlights of the show.

Jackson kicked off his first concert in four years in punchy style as he was catapulted from a trap door beneath the stage. As fireworks and golden sparks exploded all around him, he burst into what would be the fifth single from his album, 'Jam'. Explosions punctuated the show, but despite all the pyrotechnics there was no disguising the fact that much of it had been seen and done before. There were some spec-tacular moments, like when the singer danced with skeletons during 'Thriller', and some very gushy ones, like when he brought on dozens of children who paraded in front of a huge brightly lit globe for 'Heal the World'. And there is no denying that some of his songs are great pop – 'Billie Jean', 'Human Nature', 'Smooth Criminal', 'Black or White' and 'Will You Be There?' have few equals in any artist's canon. But all the hype and hullabaloo promising the most spectacular show was just so much hot air. It wasn't. And Jackson didn't interact with the crowd apart from telling them in German that he loved them all.

The two-hour show ended in true Hollywood fashion with Jackson being thrown into a huge white space-suit which then propelled him through the air back to his dressing-room. It was a stunt that James Bond would have been proud of, but it wasn't enough. Next time around Jacko shouldn't concern himself so much about making an exit, but about what comes before. If he wants to be a real 'Thriller' he should get some new ideas and some fresh sounds. He should stop worrying about the shape of his nose and start worrying about the shape of his act. Otherwise he is in danger of fast becoming old-fashioned. Right now he still possesses magic, even if much of the fairy dust he sparkled on the crowd seemed rather stale.

As he set off for Thailand and the second leg of his world tour, I wrote:

Jackson's latest album *Dangerous* and his latest gigantic tour have received much critical flak. The star has been accused of sticking too close to his winning formula and giving us a re-hash of his past glories. The sensitive superstar has been much hurt by this criticism because the stage, he has always said, is the one place he can truly feel comfortable in and where he can really come alive. That is why Jackson's current tour could be the most important of his life.

I was referring to Jackson's music and his stage show. It was a pertinent observation and I was not the only one who voiced fears over what was happening to Jackson. But those words were to be chillingly prophetic in a way nobody, then, could ever have realized.

CHAPTER 4

On With the Show

ALL THE PRESSURE caused by the allegations quickly took its toll on Jackson. Soon after the scandal broke, he did the first of his disappearing tricks. Hotel executives at Bangkok's luxurious Oriental Hotel lamely said that Jackson had disappeared because he wanted some breathing space. But things were getting to the singer both physically and mentally. Jackson cancelled the second Bangkok show from a secret location, pleading illness. He made a statement in a tape-recorded message in which, in a strangely quiet voice, he said: 'Be calm. To all my fans in Bangkok, Thailand, I am sorry for not performing yesterday as I am really sick. I am still under medical treatment and have been instructed by the doctor not to perform before Friday 27 August 1993.' He promised fans that he would not let them down and that he would do a show at the stadium within a few days.

But it was Jackson who needed calming, not the fans. Sources said that he had become anxious and depressed because of the allegations; he had locked himself in his room and refused to speak to anyone in person – only taking phone calls. From time to time he collapsed on his bed and began sobbing uncontrollably.

Jackson's health and emotional vulnerability had been a worry to his friends in the past. He was frail and often suffered panic attacks which had involved emergency visits to hospital. Some of his friends were worried that the quicksand of scandal that he found himself submerged in might drag him down into a deep depression and could lead to a complete breakdown; it was even feared that he might take his own life. Jackson's brother-in-law, LaToya's husband and manager Jack Gordon, painted a bleak picture of the singer and issued a chilling warning: 'I really think he will kill himself. I truly believe that this is how it will end. Michael is not very strong.' Movie producer Tony Pastor, said to be a very close friend of the Jacksons, revealed: 'There is deep concern within the family that Michael has never had to handle anything like this before. He has never faced revulsion and hate.'

As these suicide worries raged around Jackson, his publicist, Lee Solters, a veteran of the PR industry, immediately issued a statement which dismissed any fears of suicide attempts: 'There has been a report that Michael has tried to kill himself. I can categorically say that there is no truth whatsoever in this.'

On 27 August Jackson finally performed his Bangkok concert. It was reported that he had decided to stage the show only after the Thai government threatened to stop him leaving the country unless he performed. Before he left Bangkok, Jackson tried to get back into his old routine by shooting a pop video with 150 uniformed Thai airforce cadets. He marched alongside them wearing a bright orange shirt and tight black trousers. But even that did not go according to plan after Jackson's aides got into a row over photographing him with some of the army people.

In the midst of the maelstrom came Jackson's birthday on Sunday 29 August. There was no celebration and no cause for celebration either. It was the most miserable birthday of his life. But Jackson, who had survived thirty gruelling years in the cut-throat world of show business, was determined not to be beaten. He had a show to do and fans, who had paid good money to see him, to entertain. Forty thousand fans, who cheered him on as he performed his energetic two-hour show in the National Stadium in Singapore, the next stop on the tour, had the time of their life. Somehow Jackson had managed to muster some of that old 'Black or White' magic and summon enough energy, confidence and courage to do what he did best – perform. It was a performance which, according to local reports, electrified the crowd. To those fans who sang and danced along with the singer it looked as if he didn't have a care in the world. In spite of everything, the magic of his singing and dancing was still there.

But on the day of Jackson's second Singapore show, the troubles and worries that had been plaguing him returned, renewing once again fears that his health had been shattered by the relentless sex allegations. Minutes before he was due to go on stage, Jackson suddenly collapsed in the arms of his doctor in his dressing-room. This was the third show that he had cancelled in just seven days since the revelation of child abuse allegations.

When the announcement was made that he had been taken ill, there was a stunned silence. Most fans left the stadium, upset that Jackson could not play and worried about what was happening to him. But some became increasingly agitated and angry and the police, fearing a riot among the fans – many of whom had travelled hundreds of miles to see the show – rushed to the stage and tried to clamber on to it. Furious fans besieged the promoter's office, chanting: 'We want our money back!' while others besieged the hotel where Jackson was having his medical examination.

The singer was carried from the backstage area of Singapore's National Stadium into a darkened van and rushed back to his suite at Raffles Hotel. There he was examined by a brain specialist. Doctors said that he had been struck by a severe migraine which had left him shaking, vomiting and barely able to stand.

The local neurologist who examined him checked the superstar's eyesight and co-ordination and he was ordered to bed. David Forecast, a Harley Street specialist in migraine and gastric complaints, had flown from London to see Jackson when he was taken ill in Bangkok and was now travelling with the Jackson entourage. He painted a picture of a courageous star determined not to let down his fans as he battled against illness; at the same time he denied that Jackson's condition had been brought on by the scandal:

Mr Jackson could barely stand up but he wanted to perform against my advice. It looks as though over the last few months he has been suffering from acute vascular migraine. It was simply impossible to hold the performance tonight. I cannot have him in a situation which is a danger to him. And I cannot have him perform for two hours with a migraine when he is dizzy, nauseous and vomiting. He was well this afternoon but as we went to the stadium he slowly developed his acute headache or migraine. The headache came on slowly. I was still trying to get control of it thirty minutes before the show. In my medical opinion this illness is completely coincidental and not related to any allegations whatsoever.

The following day Jackson, in a tape-recorded message, admitted: 'I was suddenly taken ill last night. I am sorry for the cancellation of my performance. I apologize for any inconvenience it must have caused my fans in Singapore. I look forward to seeing you all at the stadium tomorrow. Thank you for your continued support and understanding. I love you all. Thank you.'

The singer was also taken to Singapore's Mount Victoria

Hospital, where he had a brain scan by MRI — magnetic resonance imagery. The scanner, which is highly accurate, requires the patient to lie still for an hour. It gives doctors a 3-D picture of the brain, a picture which can be further dissected on computer. After studying the results, Jackson was given the all-clear and allowed to perform on stage that night. Forecast, commenting on Jackson's condition, said:

> We have consulted a local expert in neurology and he has agreed with the clinical diagnoses that it is a late-onset migraine. Medication has been prescribed and we would not anticipate any further attacks. He is totally fit, and will perform. I believe it started about six weeks ago. But the news is very good. He is on a regular treatment that we use in migraines. He has commenced medication and we don't anticipate any similar problems.

Jackson's cancelled Singapore show was rescheduled for 1 September, and once again the singer managed to give the fans a show to remember.

In Taiwan, the next stop on the tour, Jackson decided to put a brave face on it. Just as he had continued to have children appear in his show, so he also continued to do all the childish things that he had become known for. He bought £3,000 worth of toys in the kind of spending spree he had loved to indulge in during the good old days when he had just been seen as a Peter Pan. To Jackson, it was the equivalent of a woman buying a parade of outfits to cheer herself up. But the toys did not weave any kind of magic spell to put a stop to his problems. The last Taiwan show was an emotional experience: four women fainted and at one point a tearful young woman ran on to the stage and hugged Jackson. At least it showed the world that his fans were still behind him.

His next port of call was Japan, a country that is a gold-mine to many Western performers, and one of the countries that Jackson is most fond of. It was here that he had kicked off his *Bad* tour – one of the greatest pop tours of all time – with a show which I attended, among the best I had ever seen.

After Japan the singer faced one of the biggest challenges of his life, playing in Moscow. Though Jackson again put on a superb performance, the whole show was not a highspot of his career. The promoters claimed that they had sold 71,000 tickets for the show, but it was attended by only 30,000 fans. The poor turn-out was blamed on the heavy rain which delayed the show for two hours and which soaked the singer, doing his first show in the former Soviet Union, as the wind lashed against the covered stage.

On Friday 17 September the singer flew to Israel to give two concerts in Tel Aviv. While he was there he visited one of the most holy places in the whole world, Jerusalem's Wailing Wall. During his walkabout, he spotted a boy in the crowd, beckoned to him and then strolled with him to the Wall. Here, at the holiest of shrines, Jackson was mobbed by hundreds of fans, and the pandemonium that ensued angered Jews who were worshipping and praying there. They threw chairs, barring the way to the shrine against Jackson and his thirty-strong entourage. The crowd, who were praying there on one of the holiest days of the year, shouted: 'Don't desecrate the Sabbath.' Jackson stood, silently holding the boy's hand, as his aides argued for him to be allowed through to the Wall, but it was all in vain and the singer was forced to retreat and be driven back to his hotel. Jackson spent the rest of the day resting before stepping on stage for what was to be Israel's largest ever rock concert.

It was after Jackson had played his next stop, Turkey, that the world tour first appeared to be seriously at risk. Ticket sales for the Australian dates, where the tour was set to finish, were halted as reports claimed that Jackson was to be forced to return to America.

Jackson performed his last concert of the *Dangerous* tour at Mexico City's El Estadio Del Azteca in front of 120,000 screaming fans. Little did any of the gigantic audience realize that soon after that performance the singer would stun the world by quitting the tour and confessing that he was addicted to painkilling drugs. Only days before Jackson decided to scrap the tour, it was claimed that there was no danger whatsoever of it being cancelled. One of his American spokesmen, answering questions on why the singer had not attended the funeral of his 100-year-old grandfather, categorically stated: 'We have no intention of leaving this tour until it is completed.' The fans who saw that show said that Jackson put on an energetic performance which belied the torment and pain he was in.

Then, in the second week of November 1993, Michael Jackson disappeared from the world. He suddenly scrapped the rest of his tour, which had another month of dates left and which at one time was set to finish in Australia, and, amidst rumours of breakdown and drug addiction, went into hiding.

As the lawyers battled it out against each other in Los Angeles and as news of the scandal raced around the world, Jackson had done his best to carry on with his tour and his aides tried to limit the amount of damage done to his career. But their task was continually plagued by setbacks and further allegations had come thick and fast: on the same day that the boys Brett and Wade had been wheeled out on TV to vouch for Jackson, his sister LaToya, the most outspoken and rebellious of the Jackson clan, revealed how she had warned her brother about his obsession with children five months previously. LaToya said she had told her brother to call a halt to his friendships with young boys. She had told him that she was concerned about his string of toy-boy pals and feared his friendships with them could wreck his career. LaToya's husband Jack Gordon, said: 'He didn't take her advice and now look what's happened. LaToya is very sorry for Michael, but she did try to warn him about all this.'

The rest of the Jackson family had finally got behind their money-spinning son on 30 August – seven days after the allegations first surfaced. They insisted the claims were a pack of lies. The family get-together took place in Los Angeles while Jackson was in Singapore. Katherine and Joe were in attendance, together with his brothers Jermaine, now thirty-nine, and Tito, forty, and his eldest sister Rebbie, forty-four. But noticeable by her absence was his sister Janet – the sibling he is said to be closest to – who was prevented from attending the conference because of a heavy work schedule.

Jackson's mother made an emotional speech in which she told the world:

> I raised my boy and I know he is innocent. First of all I would like to let the world know that I'm behind my son. I don't believe any of this stuff that is being written about him. I love him. I've talked with him several times since this has come out and I plan to go and visit him. He knows I'm coming. This is a very difficult time for us all. What makes it worse is that I know Michael would never do anything like this.

Jermaine Jackson read out a statement in which the family declared their total love and support for the star and spoke out about the help and love he had given needy children all over the world:

> We'd like to take this opportunity when our family have come together in unity and harmony to convey

our love and unfailing support for Michael. We know, as does the whole world, that he has dedicated his life to providing love and care for young people everywhere. Further, we wish to state our collective and unequivocal belief that Michael has been made the victim of a cruel and an obvious attempt to take advantage of his fame and success. His compassion for all people is legendary. Accordingly we are confident that his dignity and humanity will prevail at this most difficult time. Our entire family stand firmly at his side. We are also in the process of planning a trip for the entire family to go and see our brother to support him. It will be very soon.

Several nieces, nephews and cousins were also present at the conference, which was broadcast live on the global satellite network CNN. Around 65 million people watched in over 130 countries as far away as Fiji and Mongolia. The conference had originally been planned in order to give details of an upcoming TV special about the Jackson family's life story. But the Jacksons decided it was a perfect time to include a heartfelt defence of Michael and a pledge to stand united behind him. They later joined Michael when the tour reached Taiwan. This was the first time he had seen his family since the scandal had broken.

But only hours after Jackson's family had made their emotional defence, Evan Chandler was heard by millions attacking the singer. The threats had been recorded on tape and broadcast on the American TV station, KCBS. 'I'm going to ruin Michael's career and bring him down,' Chandler shouted. 'This whole thing is going to crash down on everybody and destroy everybody on sight. Michael has broken up the family. I will get everything I want and they will be destroyed forever. Michael's career will be over. It's irrelevant to me whether that helps Jordan.'

Chandler said he wanted custody of his son because his

When the Jackson Five appeared at a Royal Variety Show
in London in 1973, the young Michael Jackson was already
an inveterate performer.

Life for the young star was a gruelling schedule of live
shows and recording studios – many say he missed out on a
proper childhood altogether.

Bubbles the chimpanzee and a llama called Louis were two of Jackson's closest animal companions while *Off The Wall* was topping charts in the UK and the USA.

Neverland, Jackson's palatial home, complete with
fun park and a carousel which plays 'Like A Virgin'.

Jackson's parents now live in Havenhurst, the £3.5-
million house the singer bought in Encino, California
– he still has his own bedroom there.

Brooke Shields has always denied any romantic link with Jackson, although the two former child stars have been good friends for many years.

Jackson pays a visit to the 'Heal the World' orphanage in Romania in 1992.

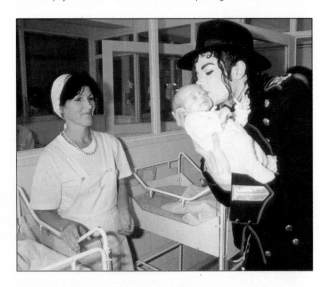

Liz Taylor is Jackson's greatest supporter and one of his biggest fans.

Jackson attends a huge party thrown for him at the Guild Hall, London, in 1988, accompanied by Jimmy Safechuck, the boy he befriended after they worked together on a Pepsi advert.

Jackson and Macaulay Culkin, pictured here in a Bermudan hotel penthouse in 1991, became friends after the child star appeared in the singer's *Black or White* video.

Eleven-year-old Brett Barnes, shown here with Jackson at EuroDisney *(above)* and in London *(right)*, agreed to appear on prime-time American TV to talk about his friendship with the singer and to protest Michael's innocence.

Ecstatic fans mob Jackson as he arrives by helicopter in London.

Jackson and his entourage are spotted leaving his London hotel during the *Dangerous* tour.

ex-wife was harming their child by allowing Jackson to have contact with him:

> If I go through with this, I go big time. I will get everything I want. The mother is going to lose Jordan and Michael's career will be over. He will not believe what will happen to him. This man will be humiliated beyond belief and I have the evidence to prove it. The mother is harming Jordan and Jackson is harming him and I can prove it. It cost me hundreds and thousands of dollars to get the information I've got and you know that I don't have that kind of money. It would be a massacre if I don't get what I want. I know Michael is bad for my son – I know what he has to hide. Michael is using his age and his experience, money and power to take advantage of Jordan. The problem is that he is greatly harming him for his own selfish reasons. He is not the altruistic kind of human being he appears to be. What will happen to him will be beyond his worst nightmare. He will not sell more than one record. The facts are so overwhelming that everyone will be destroyed in the process.

The tapes were part of a secret recording of three lengthy conversations with Evan Chandler that Jordan's stepfather, Dave Schwartz, had made in an attempt to help his wife. These tapes had been handed over to Fields and Pellicano. Jackson's camp later distributed them to the media to show what an evil character Chandler was. It was one more demonstration of the fact that the case was becoming a trial through television rather than a trial in the courtrooms.

Pellicano's thoughts behind releasing the tape – which was broadcast as Jackson cancelled his concert in Singapore – must have been to show Evan Chandler as a man desperate to destroy Jackson at all costs, even if it meant sacrificing his son to do so; as a man hell-bent on evil. But once again the Jackson team's tactics partially backfired. To many who were avidly following the scandal, the taped conversation – which had taken place the day before Chandler met Jackson – seemed to suggest that Chandler's motive was purely to get custody and *not* to blackmail Jackson for millions.

At the beginning of September it was reported that a crack police squad had been probing Michael Jackson's friendships with boys five years back, raising fears that his apparently innocent relationships with boys might have been going on for some time. While Jackson was in Japan it was said that the Los Angeles police wanted to question the singer and there were even worries that he might have to cancel more dates and return to his homeland. A police source admitted: 'The time is fast approaching when we must ask certain questions in public.'

Soon after this it was revealed that Jordan Chandler was no longer at the exclusive private school that he attended. Jordan was told not to return to St Matthew's School in Los Angeles, where such celebrities as Steven Spielberg send their children, until the scandal was over. The decision to suspend him was taken after parents complained about the number of photographers, reporters and 'sightseers' who had besieged the school in the hope of getting a glimpse of the young boy. One parent commented: 'It's been absolute murder ever since this thing broke. There are photographers, reporters, TV crews and rubbernecks everywhere. The situation has got out of hand and our children's lives have been turned upside down.'

It was also while he was in Japan that the singer got one of the first good bits of news in a scandal that seemed to be rapidly dragging him down: Jordan Chandler's new lawyer, the formidable Gloria Allred, had quit. The high-powered lawyer decided not to represent Jordan just eight days after she had told a packed news conference: 'I have taken on Jordie's case because I believe it is a worthy cause and that this child truly means to have his day in court.'

But this time she stayed silent and refused to give any reason for her decision. Instead she merely stated: 'I no longer represent the child. I can't make any further comment unfortunately.'

Jackson's lawyer, Howard Weitzman, speculated that her decision to quit may have been because Jordan Chandler's camp had been frightened by her very public approach. He said: 'I can provide no insight to why the change was made, except to say that perhaps the people involved did not want to make this a media circus. But then perhaps, maybe she didn't believe the kid.'

Allred's departure demonstrated the changeability that was a characteristic of the Chandler camp. Evan Chandler had originally hired Barry Rothman to represent him, but they parted company when Jackson's security chief, Pellicano, claimed Rothman was part of a blackmail plot. Attorney Richard Hirsch took over. Also involved at one time was private detective Ernie Rizzo, who claimed to represent the family but was later publicly disowned by Hirsch.

The news of Allred's departure was celebrated by the Jackson camp, who saw her shock withdrawal as a victory.

But, just twenty-four hours later, the singer was hit by some devastating news. Jordan Chandler had launched a multi-million-pound civil lawsuit, making a catalogue of charges against him, including sexual battery, seduction, wilful misconduct, fraud and negligence. The seventeen-page suit, which was filed at the Santa Monica Superior Court, set out in explicit sexual detail the acts which Jordan claimed Jackson had performed on him. The action claimed that Jackson had seduced Jordan into a 'despicable sexual relationship through sordid manipulation of trust and friendship.'

Unspecified compensation, punitive damages and costs were demanded. The document stated:

Defendant Michael Jackson, with the intent to cause a harmful and offensive contact with an intimate part of the plaintiff, repeatedly committed sexual battery upon plaintiff by having sexually offensive contacts with plaintiff. These sexually offensive contacts include, but are not limited to defendant Michael Jackson orally copulating plaintiff, masturbating plaintiff, having plaintiff fondle and manipulate the breasts and nipples of defendant Michael Jackson while defendant would masturbate.

In another section the papers stated:

As a direct result of the repeated sexual batteries committed by the defendant upon the plaintiff, the plaintiff has suffered injury to his health, strength and active injury to his body and shock to his nervous system . . . The defendant's actions were done with the sole and exclusive purpose of satisfying the defendant's lust and sexual desires. As a result the defendant was able to seduce plaintiff and thereby Michael Jackson was able to satisfy his lust.

It was pure dynamite. This was the first time the singer had been associated in public documents with suspected crimes previously only mentioned by innuendo and in a confidential psychiatric report.

The worry for Jackson was that if the civil case came to trial the singer would be forced to defend himself in court, legal experts revealed; if he did not he could lose by default. The lawsuit also saw Jordan Chandler's team on the offensive for the first time – up until that moment most of the information (or misinformation) released over the scandal had come from the singer's side.

But the decision of Chandler's legal aides – the respected lawyer Larry Feldman had by now replaced Gloria Allred – to sue Jackson personally in a civil lawsuit did not mean that the police investigation would be railroaded. The police could still bring a criminal prosecution against the singer if they had enough evidence. However, legal experts believed that the move had forced the hand of everyone involved in the case. Chandler's legal team had taken the initiative and bypassed the police in order to get the case to court. Larry Feldman claimed that the action was filed in an attempt to speed things up while the police were investigating the allegations against the singer. He said that he hoped to have the case, number SC026226, in court within six months: 'This child's life and emotional well-being hangs in the balance. This is the quickest way to get this kid's life back into order.' Feldman admitted that Jordan was currently undergoing extensive therapy because of what had happened to him and the attendant publicity that the allegations had brought. The action had by this time united Evan Chandler with his ex-wife, June Schwartz. Hirsch said that the action had the full support of both Jordan's parents, who had previously been extremely hostile towards each other.

A number of legal experts believed that Jordan Chandler's legal move had put Jackson in a no-win situation: if Jackson went to court and the boy repeated all the charges contained in the papers, he could be destroyed, while if he settled out of court, many people would infer that he was guilty.

But Jackson's representatives refused to be pushed into a corner. They once again dismissed the lawsuit and the allegations as an attempt by Evan Chandler to extort £13 million from the singer. Pellicano said bluntly: 'We vehemently deny all the allegations.'

The civil lawsuit put another spanner in the works. It was reported that Feldman was battling to serve a sub-poena on Jackson, demanding that he return to America to answer a whole number of questions under cross-examination, a move which would effectively wreck the remainder of Jackson's world tour. And speculation grew, after Jackson had finished playing Turkey, that the singer could be about to return home to face the child abuse allegations. Jackson's aides halted ticket sales for the Aus-tralian dates of the tour, which were due to start on 3 December. The cancellation of the Australian leg came just ten days after lawyers for Jordan Chandler demanded that he return home within a month. At the time Jackson's representatives in Australia played down the disappear-ance of the Down Under dates. They said that that had merely been postponed because Jackson wanted to restruc-ture and change his show.

Jackson was in Argentina, on the South American leg of his tour, when one of the most damaging pieces of infor-mation emerged. It was claimed that police now, after two months of solid investigation, had enough evidence to re-commend charging the singer over the sex abuse allega-tions. They were said to have informed his advisers that they were in the process of compiling sufficient evidence for the district attorney to present a case in court. Officers had even flown to Manila in their quest for evidence to interview two of Jackson's former employees, Mark and Faye Quindoy. Jackson's advisers were believed to have told him to prepare for the worst when he set foot in his homeland again. According to *National Enquirer* magazine, a source close to the investigation admitted:

> The police have enough to recommend that Jackson be charged right now, but first they want to talk to him. Michael's aides have always tried to protect him from the outside world. But when they learned that

the case was not going away, they decided to appraise him of the gravity of the situation and that, in all likelihood, he could be charged. One of the problems is that Michael is still living in a make-believe land and he thinks that no one can touch him.

Jackson's legal aides managed to win the embattled star a welcome ten-day reprieve in answering the lawsuit brought by Jordan Chandler. The deadline for Jackson to respond to the sex abuse claims was originally to have been Wednesday 13 October, but Jackson's lawyers complained that they had only had the papers in their possession for a short time and they were granted an extension.

As October drew to a close the worst fears of the Jackson camp were realized: the singer was finally ordered to return to America to answer the child sex allegations. While he was in Mexico, lawyers for Jordan Chandler served on him a notice of deposition. This demanded that Jackson return almost immediately to answer questions under oath about the allegations. Larry Feldman commented:

> Although there has been considerable movement in this case Jackson's lawyers have not yet agreed to our request. If Mr Jackson isn't here on Monday (1 November) we can then go and ask for a court order demanding his return. If he doesn't comply with that order then he will be a fugitive. If he wants to continue to appear to be a model citizen, he will have to come back.

Legal experts explained that if a court order was made, the judge would set a date for the singer to face his accuser's legal team. That hearing would be videotaped so that experts would be able to analyse Jackson's response to questions.

In a separate move, it was revealed that prosecutors had convened grand juries in four cities in case the allegations developed into a criminal trial. A police chief revealed that juries had been put on stand-by in Los Angeles, Santa Barbara, Las Vegas and Miami – in every place where Jordan Chandler alleged he had been molested by Jackson.

Jackson, however, was believed to have no plans to face the allegations, and his legal team even tried to get the multi-million-pound civil lawsuit against him postponed for six years. It was revealed that under American law the singer could delay a civil action until criminal investigations were completed, and the deadline for police to bring charges against the singer was as far away as August 1999 – six years after their investigation began. Jackson's legal move came after his lawyers grew concerned that the civil proceedings brought by Jordan Chandler could influence any potential future criminal case. But Jackson's opposition saw it as a tactic to ensure the civil case never saw the light of day. A source in the Chandler camp said: 'The legal move is a cynical attempt to make sure that the case never gets heard.'

The singer's insistence on the six-year postponement came in a seventeen-page document filed in the Los Angeles court. In that document Jackson hit back more vehemently than ever before. He denied all the sex abuse allegations against him and formally accused Evan Chandler of blackmail, claiming that he had induced his son to make 'false, defamatory and hurtful' allegations against him. He furthermore declared that those allegations were made after Evan Chandler had failed to extort £13 million from him. It was powerful stuff and just the kind of response that Jackson fans had been waiting for.

Though Jackson admitted in the statement that Jordan was his friend and that he had given expensive gifts to him, he strongly denied that any acts of sexual molestation had taken place at all: 'There was no sexual abuse or any form of abuse whatsoever.' The star also denied that he kissed and fondled the boy to satisfy his own 'lust, passion and sexual desire', and said that charges that the boy was 'damaged' by their relationship were lies.

The fears that Jackson would scrap the tour, which had been building up ever since the allegations were made in August, were finally realized in November while Jackson was in Mexico. The announcement took place just a few days after another police raid – this time on Havenhurst, the £3.5-million house in the Los Angeles suburb of Encino which the singer had bought for his parents in 1987 and of which he owned 75 per cent; Jackson had once lived there and still had a bedroom where he was alleged to have entertained dozens of young boys, sneaking them in while his parents were asleep.

During the eight-hour search, performed on 9 November while the Jackson parents were away, a dozen detectives seized six boxes of material from the house. Their search warrant stated they had the right to seize 'any photographs, slides, negatives or video recordings of male juveniles nude and/or in sexually explicit poses'.

Eleven magazines, six boxes of notebooks, photos and files were believed to have been removed from the house. A safe was also broken open to reveal a number of handwritten notes, according to a source.

Michael Jackson's famous disappearance in the second week of November 1993 took place after Los Angeles police were said to have secured a search warrant ordering Jackson to strip naked to see if the intimate marks on his body, including his genitals, matched those described to the police by Jordan Chandler. The police were said to be furious that the singer's aides had been tipped off about their plans.

The day after Jackson fled he was due to play Puerto Rico, an American protectorate, and speculation abounded that Jackson was to be questioned by the police when he landed there. And, technically, they could even have arrested the star, who had not been back to America since the allegations broke. But Jackson's legal team denied that the singer had feared arrest in Puerto Rico; they claimed that the rest of the *Dangerous* tour had been scrapped on legitimate medical grounds.

While Michael Jackson went to ground, his mother made another appearance on television. Again she told the world – through Cable Channel CNN – of her son's innocence. But she also maintained that the best way of proving that innocence was for him to come back home to America: 'I want to tell him to hang on in there and come home soon. Let the people know and prove your innocence. It seems like everything is going down a one-way street. You have to come home and defend yourself because this is the only way you can let people know you are not guilty of this.' She slammed reports which put into question her son's sexual orientation: 'Michael's appearance makes a lot of people think he is gay, but he is not. He'd never do anything like this and he never will because he is not a child molester. Even though he was in the room with these kids, they have fun. The doors weren't locked. Kids came over and had fun in the games room.'

Mrs Jackson also hit out at his legal team 'for making mistakes': she claimed that they had not defended his reputation loudly enough in public.

Meanwhile, the world continued to speculate about where Michael Jackson could be.

CHAPTER 5

Vanishing Act

At the beginning of September, in Taiwan, there had been concern about the singer's mental state, but he was given the all-clear by his doctor, Forecast, and went on to perform two shows there. Indeed, he managed to fulfil most of his engagements until he reached Mexico City in November. Here, Jackson did spend some time in the town's ABC Hospital but he was not admitted to treat his addiction to dangerous painkillers, which he was soon to confess to the world; nor was he there because of the dehydration or the migraine or the stomach pains that had caused him to cancel a number of concerts earlier on this leg of the tour. His hospital visit was brought about by the most everyday occurrence: toothache. Jackson had been struck down by an abscessed tooth which had to be pulled out. A source in the Jackson camp said at the time: 'Though the stress of the child abuse allegations had caused him to look fatigued and pressurized, he didn't look at all like he was under the influence of drugs to me. He seemed relaxed and coherent.'

But there were some hints that Jackson was having drug problems two days before he fled the country. During his time in Mexico City he spent ten hours giving video-taped testimony after two songwriters claimed he had stolen songs from them. The singer appeared sluggish and incoherent as he answered the charges. He seemed drowsy and his eyes were heavy-lidded, and he paused for long periods during his statement. He faltered when he was asked if he had written the songs and even when he was asked to name his brothers in the Jackson Five. He seemed lifeless and distracted throughout the time he spent giving his deposition, except for one moment when he came alive as he told lawyers: 'Songwriting just comes to me. It's like standing under a tree and trying to catch a leaf. It's very spiritual.'

But lawyer Howard Manning, who represented the songwriters in their case against Jackson, said he did not feel the superstar was in a drug haze: 'He performed well as a witness. He's a very bright man.'

Nevertheless, Jackson was reported to have embarked on a two-week-long drug binge while he was in Mexico City, which had ended with the singer breaking down and wrecking his hotel room. He was said to have gone berserk after taking large doses of the painkiller Percodan and the tranquillizer Valium for fourteen days, according to *National Enquirer* magazine. His rampage cost a hefty $3,000 (£2,000) to put right again. His crisis was said to have reached its climax on 8 November, which was the day the police raided his parents' home in Encino looking for evidence of child sex abuse. The singer immediately rang his close friend Elizabeth Taylor for help, telling her that he badly needed her by his side to help him get through this new ordeal.

It was while Taylor was on her way to Mexico City that Michael suffered the breakdown, it was claimed. The *Enquirer* was told by a friend of Jackson's:

Michael was convinced he'd be arrested when he reached Puerto Rico and he'd been popping Percodan like candy all day. He began to laugh hysterically and then suddenly his weird laughter turned into cries of anguish and he sobbed angrily. A few seconds later Michael began repeatedly banging his head against the living-room wall, so much so he left an indent in the white plaster. He cried out: 'Why me, why me? What are they trying to do to me? They are killing me bit by bit.' He sank to his knees, leaned forward and vomited all over the floor. A minute or so later Michael walked quietly into his bedroom where he began scribbling on the walls like a kid. But the words he scribbled didn't make any sense. Then the weirdest thing happened. Michael picked up a notepad and began writing 'I love you' over and over again. He smiled strangely and said: 'It's true, you know, I do love you, you're all my children.' Finally Michael covered his eyes with his hands and moaned, 'I can't bear any more.' He shuffled to his bed, collapsed on it and fell into a deep sleep with his knees drawn up under his chin.

Then Liz Taylor arrived and decided that Jackson needed immediate help to cure his addiction.

Other sources, however, told a completely different story: they said that the devastation wreaked on the Mexico City hotel room was not caused by a drug binge, but by children's frolics which had got out of hand. One source claimed: 'It was the kids who were scribbling all over the walls. That's why the writing was such gobbledegook.' Such conflicting stories only added to the mystery surrounding Jackson's disappearance.

Jackson's escape from Mexico City was a real cloak-and-dagger affair, and it took him around the world in a 6,000-mile air dash. It was achieved with the support and help of Elizabeth Taylor. Jackson, his head wrapped up in towels, sneaked on to a private Boeing 727, accompanied by Taylor, her husband Larry Fortenski, his security chief Bill

Bray, and a team of aides, including Bob Jones. The plane made brief stops in Canada and Iceland before landing at Britain's Luton airport around 1 a.m. Shortly afterwards, two unidentified people got off and were checked by immigration officials. After refuelling again, the plane flew on to Switzerland. Geneva airport staff say that Liz Taylor and two other passengers were driven away. Again it was hard to ascertain if Jackson was one of these passengers: in an effort to conceal their identities, all three were, according to sources, wrapped up from head to foot in duffel-style coats, with hoods pulled right down over their faces and dark sunglasses concealing their eyes. The airport staff could not even tell if they were male or female.

Jackson was never once sighted by the public during his four-week disappearance. Reports claimed that he arrived at the Charter Nightingale Clinic in Marylebone, London, during the early hours of that Saturday morning in November. There he was met by Beauchamp Colclough, the specialist who was put in charge of weaning Jackson off his addiction to powerful painkillers, among them a drug called DF–118. The medical team treating the singer was said by sources to have broken his addiction by withholding the painkilling drugs and sedating him with the tranquillizer Valium to help him cope with the withdrawal. This treatment left Jackson totally dazed and confused. He was then weaned off Valium until his body did not need any medication at all. A member of staff at the clinic said: 'Mr Jackson is heavily under the influence of Valium. He is more or less incoherent. The amount of Valium will be gradually reduced until he begins to feel better once more.'

While the world hunted for him, Michael Jackson put out a taped statement about his condition and his decision to cancel the remainder of his *Dangerous* tour through his American publicist. The singer said that he had become addicted to painkillers because of recent reconstructive scalp surgery. This had become necessary following burns which Jackson had suffered during an explosion on a Pepsi commercial set over a decade ago. In a thin, shaky voice, the troubled Jackson admitted that he had become addicted to the painkilling medication that had been prescribed for him:

> Seven months ago I had major reconstructive surgery on my scalp, which was burned filming a TV commercial. I was prescribed medication due to the severe pain caused by the operation. These medications were taken sparingly at first and it had no effect on my ability to perform when I began this tour. As I left on the tour I was the target of an extortion attempt and shortly thereafter I was accused of horrifying and outrageous conduct. I was humiliated, embarrassed, hurt, and suffering great pain in my heart. The pressure resulting from these false allegations, coupled with the incredible energy necessary for me to perform, caused so much distress that it left me physically and emotionally exhausted. I became increasingly more dependent on the painkillers to get me through the days of my tour. My friends and doctors advised me to seek professional guidance immediately in order to eliminate what has become an addiction. It is time for me to acknowledge my need for treatment in order for me to regain my health. I realize that completing the tour is no longer possible and I must cancel the remaining dates. I know I can overcome the problem and will be stronger from the experience. I became increasingly more dependent on painkillers to get me through the tour.

The star added a message of love and hope to all the fans who had been worrying about him: 'Thank you all for your support and understanding. I shall see you soon and I love you all. Goodbye.'

But despite Jackson's message to his fans, many of them became distraught over his claims that he was severely addicted to painkilling drugs. Hundreds of fans phoned the singer's British fan magazine, *Off the Wall*, in tears, many sobbing that they wanted to end it all. As the beleaguered pop singer went deeper into hiding, his fans were desperate to find out about his condition. *Off the Wall*'s editor, Gloria Haydock, said:

We have been besieged by calls. Michael has such faithful fans and a number of them are taking this so badly they are threatening to kill themselves. Fans feel completely helpless about what is happening to Michael, they are worried sick. They are crying down the phone. We are a magazine devoted to Michael and we are here for the fans. What we are telling fans who are endangered is not to let this get on top of them, and to start looking at Michael's problems positively. We tell them that Michael has recognized the problem of his drug addiction and is getting himself healthy again. We also tell them that Michael would never want any of his fans hurting themselves over him.

Haydock gathered Jackson's fans together shortly after his announcement for a fan convention in London, explaining: 'Many of Michael's fans feel isolated and this will give them a chance to get together.'

Two days after Jackson's round-the-world flight from Mexico City, the superstar's lawyers held a press conference. Here they elaborated on Jackson's admission of his addiction. Jackson's lawyer, Bertram Fields, claimed that it was threatening the singer's life; he was so messed up by the pills he had been taking that he was 'barely able to function on an intellectual level', or even to speak. Fields said that the singer would stay in a European drug clinic which had been recommended by Liz Taylor for six to eight weeks until he was better.

The lawyer also denied that the star had sought help from a European clinic to avoid returning to the United States of America, or that he was running away from US police:

> He is not hiding out. We intend to try the criminal case and plead our innocence. The painkillers Michael was addicted to were very, very heavy-duty drugs, very, very strong. Treatment in a European clinic was chosen because there is no way we could have kept an American location a secret. We would have had helicopters flying over and fans parachuting in. Once he is cured, he will fly back to America . . . Avoiding criminal proceedings has nothing to do with this development [i.e. his addiction]. Michael Jackson has campaigned against drug addiction all his life. For him to admit he is addicted to painkillers has caused him great humiliation.

During the conference Fields was asked why Jackson had given a ten-hour legal deposition on videotape to lawyers just a week before he cancelled his tour – lawyers who said the singer seemed to be 'normal and rational'. Fields countered: 'The Michael I saw in Mexico was intellectually and intelligently impaired and I advised him not to do it. But that trial is soon to come to court and he went ahead.'

Jordan Chandler's lawyer, Larry Feldman, said when he heard the news about Jackson: 'It certainly seems that Michael Jackson is running away. The Betty Ford Clinic, which is one of the great drug rehab centres in the world, is very close to his home in Southern California. And what does Jackson do? He mysteriously gets on a plane and escapes to Europe. I find that very, very curious.'

Feldman's incredulous reaction to Jackson's claim that he was addicted to painkillers was echoed by many others. Some people believed that the whole episode was simply a scam devised to put off the moment when the singer finally had to set foot on American soil and risk arrest. Many found it hard to believe that Jackson was addicted to drugs. Drugs had always been anathema to him and was he not, after all, one of the world's most hypochondriacal stars? – a star who was fanatical about his health? He employed a chef to cook his special macro-biotic meals because he believed the human body was a temple and should be nourished only by pure food. He was a health freak who dosed himself with vitamins, and he even fasted for one day a week to cleanse and purify his system.

Another factor that fuelled people's doubts about Jackson's addiction was his ability, at what was meant to be his darkest hour, to negotiate a very important deal – the largest of its kind in history: the transfer of his music publishing company to EMI Music, a five-year agreement, for which he received £52 million. Sources close to the star said that, despite the scandals around him and his apparent drug addiction, he was shrewd and together enough to keep abreast of the negotiations and meetings with Thorn EMI. This deal was reported two weeks into Jackson's treatment for painkiller addiction. It demonstrated just what an able businessman he is, and it did not tally with the picture his lawyers were painting of him as a man who could barely speak or function, a man whose life was in danger because of his addiction.

Whether or not his addiction was as desperate as it was painted, many saw it as a great piece of positive publicity for Jackson. Not only did it temporarily stem the flood of allegations, rumours and discussions about the singer's misconduct, but it cleverly portrayed him as the victim.

When the whole scandal around Jackson blew up, it was, of course, thirteen-year-old Chandler who was seen as the victim. Now, by revealing his desperate life-threatening addiction, Jackson had, in one swiftly executed manoeuvre, taken over that role for himself. I said as much when I went on Canadian TV to discuss Jackson's flight to Europe: 'Jackson's addiction could be seen by the more cynical as a wonderful red herring to lure people away from the most important issue – did he or did he not abuse a thirteen-year-old boy? It also gave him more sympathy than at any other time since the whole affair began.'

Many people refused to see him as a naive victim. Suspicious Jackson-watchers even claimed that, while he was hiding out in Europe, the singer could be undergoing a minor operation on his genitals to get rid of distinguishing marks which Jordan had identified during the police investigation, but this was pure speculation.

Medical doubts were also cast on his addiction. One doctor said that the drugs he was supposed to have been taking – Dihydrocodeine/Benzodiazepine – were not as strong as they had been made out: 'It is interesting. These painkillers aren't as dangerous as opiates such as heroin – although a mix of them could be extremely dangerous.' Another doctor saw his addiction claims as a psychological cry for help: 'Overdosing on anything can be dangerous – if stretched to the extreme, water could be fatal. It could be a highly calculated move, but equally it could just look calculated to a cynic.'

Whatever the extent of Jackson's addiction, he did receive treatment while he was in Europe. It was the flamboyant pop star, Elton John, who had recommended to Elizabeth Taylor that Jackson should use therapist Beauchamp Colclough to cure his addiction. Elizabeth Taylor and Elton John had got to know each other well on what had become known as the International Aids Celebrity Circuit – both are partners of the AIDS Crisis

Trust which raises funds for AIDS research and sufferers. The two have met on numerous occasions since 1987, when Elton's manager John Reid held a private dinner at his Hertfordshire mansion to raise money on behalf of the London Lighthouse, a hospice for gay men. They met again two years ago at a lunch in a smart London restaurant given by Marguerite Litman, the founder of ACT. Although Elizabeth Taylor's evangelism was fuelled by her own recovery from alcoholism, it was the death of Rock Hudson from AIDS which gave it a purpose – a purpose which she has tirelessly pursued.

When Elton recommended Beauchamp Colclough, he was speaking from personal experience: he himself had been addicted to drugs and booze, and Colclough had managed to save his life by weaning him off both. Colclough, often nicknamed Beechy, is much respected by other top doctors and patients. His greatest advantage is the fact that he has been an addict himself. The forty-four-year-old Irishman had his first drink when he was twelve. It was an illegal brew that was sold in his home town of Belfast and was dubbed 'Journey into Space'. The son of an alcoholic father, Colclough also sought refuge in drink – any drink he could get hold of, including methylated spirits, surgical spirit and even aftershave. He ended up living as a down and out on the streets for three years, and was admitted to psychiatric hospitals four times.

Colclough managed to quit drinking in 1983 after a friend took him to a group therapy session for addicts. A year later he was training to be a counsellor and four years from the time he stopped drinking he was working at the renowned Promis Recovery Centre in Devon. He commented on the clinic: 'I have seen people come back from the dead at this clinic. I hear the fear of my patients and I am willing to go back with them to where it hurts to guide them out. I don't judge them or break their confidentiality.'

The treatment that Colclough uses to help his patients beat their addiction is no kid-glove affair. During a course of psychotherapy Jackson would have had to confess his innermost fears. Colclough would have explored his personality and his psyche in minute detail, asking questions about his emotions, his sexual fantasies and his life-style. Jackson would also have been made to talk about his friendships with young boys. But he would not have had to worry about anything being divulged because Colclough guarantees that everything that passes between him and his patients is in the strictest confidence.

Michael Jackson's hide-and-seek European jaunt took him to a number of different hiding places to avoid the media, who were desperate to find out where he had been secreted. One refuge was the Manor Farm Estate at Brown Candover in Hampshire, a remote country mansion owned by millionaire property tycoon Jack Dellal. Jackson was taken there just a week after he had been booked into the Charter Clinic.

Dellal confirmed: 'I was asked by the staff of the Charter Clinic whether I would let Michael Jackson stay in my country house while he underwent treatment. I was happy to help. I received no payments and did not meet him.'

It is believed that Jackson was taken by helicopter into the country shortly after his Boeing 727 touched down at Luton airport on 13 November. There are two houses on the estate, which is protected by a twelve-foot wall, electronic gates and an elaborate security system. One is a Tudor home and the other a modern house, which is where Jackson stayed.

The choice of Dellal's hideout home as a refuge for Jackson was no accident. Jack Dellal's family had itself been hit by drug addiction: one of his daughters, Suzy, had died of a heroin overdose at the age of twenty-five. Beechy Colclough first met Jack Dellal when they both became involved in charity work and subsequently became a friend of the family's.

Guy Dellal told the *Mail on Sunday*:

> Yes, he was here. I lent my house to him as a favour to my friend Beechy Colclough. I know the man through various charities I was involved in. I never met Jackson while he was here. I was asked to keep away. I wasn't involved at all – except to lend him my house – and my father was even less involved. He's a man of seventy and he's hardly interested in Michael Jackson.

The staff at Manor Farm all had to sign confidentiality agreements to stop them giving out the smallest snippet of information about the star they found in their midst. This was *de rigueur* in the Jackson camp, who are paranoid about letting stories – even the slightest piece of gossip – about the superstar leak out. But one employee did say: 'My wife and I looked after him. We went and bought his favourite foods and cooked them for him. He's definitely a Peter Pan, but I don't know if he needs therapy as much as just a lot of affection and a bit of mothering, like my wife could give him.' Jackson, who stayed at the house with his aides and security men, apparently helped with a number of household chores: hoovering was his favourite.

Elton John's beautiful mansion in Windsor was another of Jackson's bolt-holes. After that he was believed to have been transferred to a clinic in Switzerland near Elizabeth Taylor's chalet in Gstaad.

Almost two weeks after he had begun treating Michael Jackson, Beechy Colclough revealed that the detoxification programme was complete. He was speaking out, he said, because he wanted to refute categorically any suggestion that Jackson was hiding out and trying to escape from the law. It was also said that, by finally going public, Colclough was dismissing the speculation that Jackson might be hiding in order to undergo skin surgery to remove the identifying marks. Colclough's statement declared:

Mr Michael Jackson was presented to me by Dr David Forecast and Ms Elizabeth Taylor after their trip from Mexico City. With Dr Brian Wells, a consultant psychiatrist in attendance, an initial assessment of Jackson's condition was made. A detoxification programme was completed today. After an initial thirty-six hours, Mr Jackson started an intensive programme of group therapy and one-to-one therapy with myself. I anticipate Mr Jackson will complete the programme in approximately six to eight weeks as treatment solely for his dependency to painkiller medication. He remains under my care with Dr Brian Wells and Dr David Forecast in attendance. His condition is greatly improved and I confirm that no other medical, surgical or psychological condition exists. His sole problem relates to analgesia medication. I present this statement to strongly refute any suggestion that Mr Jackson is hiding out or seeking any other care other than the programme for analgesia abuse.

Inevitably, rumours abounded while the singer was in hiding: Jackson insiders in Los Angeles told me that one of the options the star was considering was moving to Switzerland: 'We were told by someone very high up in the Jackson organization that Michael had gone to ground in Switzerland. We were also told to be on alert the whole time for a change in plan.' A source in Los Angeles added:

The word here is that Michael wants to live in Switzerland now. It is the perfect getaway for him. The homes and clinics there are remote and hard to reach and the Swiss are very discreet people. They don't go around blabbing. It is a country that has more excellent clinics dotted around than any other, especially around Lausanne. A lot of people here wouldn't be surprised if Michael recreated his whole Neverland ranch there. Neverland is a fairytale place and Switzerland is the most fairytale of all countries. But Jackson's disappearance has upset a lot of people. A lot of people who were sticking up for Michael before are beginning to have doubts about his disappearance like this. And lots of people have been saying that he might never come back to America . . . Much of the speculation that he is in London and Liz Taylor flying out of Switzerland are smokescreen tactics to put people looking for Jackson off the scent. A number of showbiz folk here believe that Liz Taylor could soon be questioned by the police. She could be seen as helping a suspected felon.

Despite such suspicions, on 12 December, just a month after he had disappeared from the world in Mexico City, Jackson was back in America. His return was believed to be part of a deal struck with child abuse investigators to allow him to return home for Christmas, his favourite time of the year – the time that all children love best. Wearing a red mask and red overcoat, a mystery man said to resemble the star arrived at California's Santa Barbara airport on a private jet which was thought to have flown in from Europe via Canada. After landing the singer was whisked away to his Neverland ranch – the first time he had been back there for five months.

Reports in the New York papers said that Jackson had decided to fly back to America after winning a number of important concessions. The hush-hush operation was organized after Howard Weitzman was given an assurance that an arrest warrant would not be slapped on the star the minute he returned back home. There were also to be no 'sealed' charges against him – indictments prepared before he had the chance to tell his story. And finally he would not be taken to a police station. In exchange, Jackson was believed to have agreed to a body search to reveal whether or not Jordan Chandler was telling the truth about certain distinctive and readily identifiable markings on Jackson's body and genitalia.

Michael Jackson had made one dramatic bid to railroad the civil suit, when it was claimed that he offered Jordy Chandler a £7-million settlement. Under the terms of the deal the boy would have to agree to drop his lawsuit. Jackson's lawyer hoped that if Jordan accepted the money, the more serious criminal investigation against him could be avoided, and with that the possibility of a jail term – the thought of which had haunted the singer every day since the allegations hit the headlines. An unconfirmed story in *National Enquirer* magazine revealed:

Michael is tentatively moving to end the boy's civil case with a settlement of $10 million – the amount he's being sued for. His lawyers are quietly offering the boy that amount of money through intermediaries. They've passed word to his attorneys and are waiting a response. If it is positive then a formal offer will be made. A settlement would help the boy in taking care of his future needs – and help Michael by making it more difficult for the prosecutors. The down side is that by doing this, Michael will be admitting some sort of guilt.

The *Enquirer* also claimed that Jackson's lawyers met with Los Angeles district attorney Lauren Weiss to hammer out a plea bargain in a possible criminal case. Jackson's newly appointed lawyer, Johnnie Cochran, was rumoured to have offered a plea of guilty to a misdemeanour of unwanted touching and placing a child in a position of possible harm. This was a much lesser charge than the felony of sexual molestation, which could carry with it an eight-year prison sentence. In return the singer would agree to psychological counselling and pay a hearing fine.

But a few days later his bid was rejected. Lawyers were told: 'Keep your money, we'll see you in court.' One source claimed that Jordan Chandler's lawyer, Larry Feldman, had first been contacted by a middleman about a possible settlement in November. A few days later the £7-million deal was offered. It was claimed: 'If a deal was struck there could be some doubt that Jordan had exaggerated certain things – and that charge that his family were in it for the money would return. But you have to weigh that up against the awful pressure and ordeal of putting a young boy in court and bombarding him with probing and often hostile questions.'

On 23 December Jackson's high-powered and costly defence team was ripped apart when it was revealed that the singer's lawyer, Bertram Fields, and his private investigator, Anthony Pellicano, were no longer on the case. Sources close to the investigation claimed that both men – who had aggressively defended Jackson – had been sacked for mishandling the case. Fields's slip-up occurred when he mistakenly told a judge that a Santa Barbara county grand jury had been summoned for the criminal investigation. In fact nobody knew for sure at that time whether such a grand jury had ever been convened. Fields announced that an eight-person jury had been convened at Santa Barbara, adding: 'It's most likely that an indictment will follow.' But outside the courts Fields said he had been mistaken: 'What we understood to be the case is that subpoenas have been issued for two witnesses to appear for a grand jury proceeding in Santa Barbara county. It may very well be that the grand jury was summoned but has not yet been empanelled. We aren't always exactly sure when an indictment will take place.' Many people saw this as a ploy to postpone the civil suit – on the grounds that Jackson's legal team needed time to deal with a criminal case. If that was the case, it had backfired badly and cast doubt on Jackson's innocence. It was claimed that the detective and Jackson parted company because he had been accused of threatening certain witnesses against Jackson.

Overall, the case had not looked good for Jackson. And as the scandal ran its devastating course, a host of further allegations of child molestation had been brought to light.

CHAPTER 6

Dangerous Revelations

Towards the end of August 1993 a British disc jockey had come forward and made some startling revelations about Michael Jackson that added credence to Jordan Chandler's allegations. Terry George alleged that when he was thirteen Jackson had made some obscene phone calls to him. George had met Jackson when, as an autograph-mad schoolboy, he had managed to interview the star in his home town of Leeds. He said that they had become friends and spoke a number of times on the phone – often in the dead of night. Their most intimate conversation came when Jackson, who was then twenty, asked George in graphic detail about his sexual activities. As he questioned him Jackson told the shocked boy that he was playing with himself on the other end of the line. George told the *Mail on Sunday*: 'He just came straight out with his questions. I felt embarrassed and awkward. I didn't really understand what he was talking about. I tried to steer him off the subject and he told me: "Do you believe I'm doing it now?"'

George said that he tried to renew his friendship with Jackson four years later, in 1983, but the star's entourage prevented him from doing so. He admitted: 'I felt used because he had wanted my friendship when I was just a boy. Now I was a young man he didn't seem to want to know . . . If it hadn't been for that call I would never have believed that the allegations were possible. But when I heard the news I immediately felt part of it all.'

The next blow came from someone who had been on Jackson's staff. The former manager of his Neverland estate, Mark Quindoy, who together with his wife Faye had worked at Jackson's ranch for three years, told how he had watched Jackson put his hand in a nine-year-old boy's pants as they sat by a jacuzzi. He also claimed he saw the singer kiss a seven-year-old on the lips and caress a three-year-old.

Jackson was determined to scotch these claims. In September, while he was in Israel, he walked hand-in-hand with a young boy, thus making a visual statement to the world that his friendship with young children was not tainted by any sexual lust. And as September drew to a close Jackson refused to let the child molestation allegations change his behaviour. The children that had become his life were still in evidence around him. Despite the prosecution warnings, he spent the night under the same roof as two of his favourite young boy pals, Frank Cascio, who was thirteen, and his nine-year-old brother Eddie, in Liz Taylor's beautiful ski chalet in Gstaad, Switzerland. The next day he forked out hundreds of pounds for the youngsters when he went on a huge spending spree, buying ski suits, video games and winter clothes. Some reports said that Jackson had spent as much as £30,000 on gifts for the boys. It seemed just like the good old days when Jackson would treat his friends to anything they wanted without a care in the world.

Jackson, who was on a week's break from his world tour at the time, arrived at Taylor's chalet with the boys and their father, Dominic, in a red Chrysler Voyager. The boys' father was adamant in his defence of the beleaguered singer, insisting that Jackson was not guilty of the allegations that had been made against him: 'Michael would never harm children. He loves them.' The boys spent a total of four days holed up with Jackson in the chalet. The holiday was brought to an abrupt end when the police swooped. After their getaway break, the boy's father and also their mother, Concetta, were questioned by the police in a session which lasted eight hours.

Exactly why Jackson was still parading around with children in the midst of the scandal left most Jackson-watchers bemused. Some said it was just the singer carrying on as normal, determined not to be beaten by the allegations; others believed that he was cocking a snook at authority because he was convinced he was all-powerful and invincible; while others thought he was making a mis-judgement. Jackson's sister LaToya said she was surprised to learn of the trip. Her husband, Jack Gordon, commented: 'It just created the wrong impression.'

In October, as his lawyers were winning him his stay of execution, Jackson was in Brazil, again playing with young boys. He was said to have pitched a massive tent in his hotel room and engaged in water-pistol fights with the three young boys. This news gave his millions of fans around the world hope that the singer was back to normal – or at least what he considered normal.

From 24 October to 11 November Jackson was playing in Mexico City and staying at the Hotel Presidente, where he occupied the presidential suite on the forty-second floor. During that time he often went out on the town and once turned up at a record store with three young boys, aged between eight and thirteen, in tow. Wearing a black jacket, black fedora and black pants, he spent an hour in the Mix-up record store in the swish Pabellon Polanco shopping mall, where he bought $4,000 (£2,500) worth of CDs and laser discs. Jackson even danced and moon-walked in the back of the store with his young companions, two of whom wore outfits almost identical to his own. Once again, Jackson seemed to be making a point by refusing to let the allegations stop his friendships with young boys; conceivably he had even been advised that to put such friendships on hold would point the finger of guilt at him.

It was while he was playing the Scarlet Pimpernel of pop that Jackson was hit by yet another bombshell. In late November, as he was hiding out to try to cure himself of what he alleged was an addiction to painkillers, five of the star's former security guards sued him.

The five guards – Morris Williams, Leroy Thomas, Aaron White, Donald Starks and Fred Hammond – were suing Jackson for unfair dismissal. They alleged – in papers filed in the Los Angeles Superior Court – that the singer often spent nights alone with small boys after bringing them home at all hours of the night. The guards said that they were sacked in February 1993 because they had witnessed Jackson's night-time frolics with young boys. They claimed that the singer never had any adult friends come to his parents' Encino home and never had a girlfriend stay overnight.

Leroy Thomas later discussed the allegations more fully in an interview with the American TV programme, 'Hard Copy':

> I'd say there are about twenty kids not including the thirteen-year-old boy [a reference to Jordan Chandler], who stayed overnight. He [Mr Jackson] would have celebrity kids over and he would ask us to open up the games room. I don't know what goes on in his room but when you look at a grown man sitting with a kid in a jacuzzi, it will make you think why would you want to do that? On one occasion they all stayed all night. They were all kids.

These boys, among them *Home Alone* star, Macaulay Culkin, apparently regularly spent the night with Jackson.

In the detailed documents the guards said that Jackson engaged in all kinds of elaborate precautions to make sure his parents were unaware that the children were staying overnight:

> On some occasions Jackson would telephone to find out if his parents were home or away, or if at home if they had retired for the night. If they were gone he would then arrive alone with a young boy, typically between nine and fourteen years of age.
>
> Upon arrival at the grounds, he would drive to an area near his suite and then disappear with the boy into his suite sometimes for several hours, sometimes for the entire night.
>
> On at least one occasion he secreted a young Asian boy in the guard shack instructing the plaintiffs to keep the boy until Jackson later called for him. After Jackson's parents left the premises he called to have the boy escorted to his room.

One of the claims was that Jackson personally ordered Leroy Thomas to destroy a Polaroid picture of a naked youngster that the singer kept in his bathroom at Havenhurst:

> Jackson told Thomas that he would have to do a special assignment for him. Jackson specifically ordered Thomas to go into the family home and locate a key hidden under the refrigerator. He was then to take the key to Jackson's suite of rooms and use the key to enter Jackson's private bathroom. There Thomas was to recover a Polaroid picture of a naked young male and destroy it. Thomas did as he was ordered – and located a picture of a young male believed to be between ten and fourteen years of age. The naked male appeared to be Caucasian or possibly Asian. The photograph was a profile shot of the

young man revealing his genitals and buttocks from a side view. Thomas then attempted to destroy the photo in accordance with the instructions received from Jackson. Subsequently Jackson called and enquired if Thomas had performed his assignment. Thomas advised him that his orders had been complied with.

The guards claimed there was a huge cover-up plan to hide Jackson's obsession with young boys. The legal papers also stated that as far back as January 1993 – before Jackson had started his relationship with Jordan Chandler – the singer and his camp were aware that 'serious allegations about child molestation' were looming. The guards claimed they decided to sue despite all kinds of threats from Jackson's aides: their phones had been bugged and private eye Anthony Pellicano had been instructed to dig into their past and spy on them. They also said that they had been harassed by the singer's lawyers to 'obstruct, impede and if possible prevent any investigation or enquiry dealing with allegations that Jackson had sexually molested any young boys'. The alleged goal was for them to be painted 'disgruntled employees' to discredit anything they said. According to the guards, this was a well-tried ploy which had already been used on previous occasions when dealing with other ex-staff.

Jackson's attorney, Bertram Fields, hit back at the guards' allegations: 'Nobody was ever fired by Mr Jackson for knowing too much about anything. If they were laid off it was for an entirely different reason.'

One of the boys the guards said they had seen slipping into Jackson's bedroom was John Lennon's son Sean, who at one time had become close to Jackson. They said he would climb up the spiral staircase to Jackson's room without the singer's parents knowing. But Jackson's mother Katherine denied there was anything improper going on between them. She told the TV programme, 'Hard Copy', which had interviewed Thomas: 'Sean would come and visit and stay about a week. He was about ten. He was dropped off and Michael wasn't home. Michael ordered for him to be allowed to stay there until he got back. We weren't there . . . Michael is not a child molester. The doors to his bedroom weren't locked. Nothing went on. Do they think I am blind to what went on?' She said she had decided to go on television because she could no longer stay silent after hearing what Michael's guards were saying: 'It's time for somebody to speak up for Michael.'

In another televised interview − this time with Ted Turner's CNN network − Jackson's mother said: 'The security guards worked from our home. They were not his personal bodyguards. They were just security. A lot of the accusations they are making are not true and they know they are not true. They are saying this for the money after they were let go.'

But later there was further corroboration of the guards' claims regarding Jackson's relationship with John Lennon's son. Janet Jackson's ex-husband, singer James De Barge, who lived at the Jacksons' family home for three years, claimed that he had seen strange goings-on between Jackson and Sean. De Barge said that Sean's mother, Yoko Ono, innocently dropped her son off to stay with Jackson for a week at a time and assumed that the youngster was staying in a guest room. Instead of which he actually slept with the singer. De Barge said he had seen them in bed together: 'It was John Lennon's kid. Not Julian, the little kid Sean. The kid slept with Michael. My room was next door. I saw them when I was snooping. He knew it too. But he didn't care. I guess he figured out I was no threat.'

De Barge told of Michael's bedtime sessions with Sean Lennon during a series of allegations he made to a police informant, who secretly taped the lengthy meeting. The tape reveals further allegations by De Barge:

> I saw him running naked with another boy. It was a rainy night. I wasn't supposed to be there and I found him running naked with a boy. All the boys would sleep in his bed with him. He had all the boys over to the house to audition for his videos, more than he needed. If you went near his room when he was with them, he'd say: 'We're practising.' He didn't want anyone watching.

But on many occasions, according to De Barge, Jackson would let his guard drop and become careless about the boy friends who were coming to visit: 'He got away with it so many times he became comfortable. After doing it so many times, you feel like you don't have to hide any more. He did it right in front of me. He knew I saw him, and that I knew he was doing it, but he just kept on doing it. He trusted me.' Jackson's mother had apparently once questioned her son, having found in a drawer a $1-million cheque which the singer had made out to one of his play-mates. De Barge alleged: 'His mother confronted him about it. Michael said, "Mum, he needed help, I was just helping him." She said, "Michael, you can't be helping people like that." I don't know if it was for the kid or the parents. But I do know it was some kind of pay-off. You don't give someone a million dollars because they need it.'

De Barge believes Jackson needs serious psychiatric counselling and says he reckons Jackson's obsession with young boys is rooted in his childhood: 'Michael is what he is because of what happened to him as a kid. He is living in denial. The whole family is living in denial.'

After the guards' allegations, another of Jackson's ex-employees — the singer's former personal maid, Blanca Francia — took her courage in both hands and spoke out against him. She said that what had made her come forward was her concern about her young son's relationship with Jackson. El Salvador-born Francia, a single parent who had worked for Jackson for five years, said that on one occasion she had discovered Jackson and her son in a sleeping bag together. On another occasion she found her son sitting on Jackson's lap and even saw the singer 'rocking and rubbing' against the boy. She claimed that the singer gave her son £200 after the sleeping-bag incident on condition that he did not tell anybody.

A few months after this allegation was leaked, the maid came out with even more amazing revelations. Her claims were made in a statement to Jordan Chandler's lawyer, Larry Feldman, in December 1993. Francia, who resigned from the Jackson staff in June 1991 because she 'could no longer tolerate what was going on', described his elaborate alarm system which warned him when someone was approaching his bedroom.

She also revealed: 'One time he says to me, "Don't be surprised if you see any dirty underwear because sometimes I can't hold on to go to the bathroom and I will just go in my underwear." It was stained sometimes.' She also said that Jackson had pictures of semi-naked boys and an instant camera in his room, while his closet had videotapes and pictures of children in it.

Jackson had apparently tried to buy her silence:

He once said to me, 'What do you think about these boys coming to my house?' I said, 'It's none of my business.' And he said, 'Good.' He gave me money. He would give me five hundred, three hundred and two hundred dollars just like that. All together he gave me five thousand dollars. He gave me different stories as to why he was giving me the money – saying that I was doing a good job. He asked me to keep the visits secret. He told me that what I see is none of anybody's business and that he liked me. He said if I was asked by anyone about it, not to tell anyone about it.

Francia, a bespectacled, homely looking woman, told 'Hard Copy':

Sleeping with young boys was normal for him. I used to find boys' underwear in his bath tub. That's not normal. But it became a routine – like when I would see him lying in a bed or in a sleeping bag with young boys. And I saw mothers taking their boys to his house. He'd sleep with them for days and they'd take baths and showers together. I got to see his room where their undershorts would be on the floor together.

The entertaining of young boys had escalated once Jackson moved out of the family home in Encino, where the singer had lived with his parents until he was twenty-nine, and into his Neverland ranch. Francia, who said that the boys' parents had turned a blind eye to Jackson's behaviour because of his unlimited generosity, alleged:

It really changed once he moved to Neverland. It was like 'Now I can do what I want.' There were more young boys who were staying over longer. Sometimes the parents would come to the ranch with them but they were left on the side. They'd sleep in their own room – while the boys would sleep with Michael. I think the parents just looked away as long as they were getting money and other things. Michael always had me lie for him. When he went to his hideaway condominium in Century City he told me not to tell anyone where it was. When I asked him: 'What if your mother wants to know?' he said, 'Tell her you don't know.' That was his favourite phrase.

Michael Jackson's former chef, Johnny Ciao, who was in his employment for eighteen months, also turned against the star. He revealed that Jackson spent weekends in his bedroom and secret playroom with boys as young as seven. A whole wall of Jackson's bedroom was apparently plastered with photos of cute little boys. The chef told *National Enquirer* (the magazine which first reported the bizarre friendship that had sprung up between Jackson and Jordan Chandler): 'Nearly every weekend when Michael was at home at his California ranch there was a young boy staying over alone with him. Their ages ranged from seven to fourteen. They were all of a certain type – angelic faces, brown hair and big eyes.' Ciao caught Jackson practically naked one day when he was delivering food for the star and a thirteen-year-old companion to the door of the playroom: 'I was walking away when something made me look around – and there was Michael, naked except for a pair of white underpants. I was shocked. Michael quickly picked up the tray and went back to the room. He never acknowledged seeing me.'

Ciao said he became suspicious that something was terribly wrong when one boy's parents came to get their son because they were concerned about what was going on between him and Jackson: 'It was obvious they were very unhappy and that words had been exchanged between them and Michael. After they left with their son Michael looked very disturbed. He went to his room, didn't call me for food that night, and didn't come out until noon the following day ... What I witnessed was not the behaviour of a normal, healthy man. It was all very bizarre and unhealthy.'

Jackson's attorney, Howard Weitzman, refuted the chef's allegations, saying they were pure invention.

The next piece of bad news came from a Los Angeles TV station, which reported that a second boy had come forward publicly and accused the singer of molesting him. Though the allegations were not as damning as those made by Jordan Chandler, they nevertheless lent support and corroboration to the original accusations. The second boy was described by a source close to the investigation as being 'credible', though the Jackson camp refuted this.

Around the time that Jackson's ex-maid Blanca Francia was making allegations, another devastating piece of news surfaced. Two young boys who were being questioned by the Los Angeles police were claiming that the singer had molested them. The allegations were reported in National Enquirer, and sources close to the investigation believed that the new evidence added strength and credibility to the allegations against Jackson. If the boys testified in court, their claims could send Jackson to jail. Gerald Arenberg, chief executive officer of the National Association of Chiefs of Police, told the magazine: 'Mr Jackson is in deep trouble. If more children have come forward and told the police they have been sexually molested by Michael Jackson, this will be totally devastating to any attempt he'll make to defend himself.'

Yet another Jackson ex-employee came forward to tell about the singer's obsession with young boys. The star's former top secretary, Orietta Murdoch, revealed on 'Hard Copy' how she was warned against Jackson by his personal assistant, Norma Staikos: 'Norma Staikos took me to one side and told me not to leave my boy alone with Michael.' The secretary also claimed that the singer booked parents of the young boys he played with into secret hotels across the road from where he stayed with their children and even bought one set of parents a house and another a Mercedes. Her duties had included buying men's and boys' underwear. Orietta, who was fired by Jackson's executive secretary over a pay dispute, says she knew 'for years' what was going on between Jackson and young boys and hadn't spoken out before now because she didn't think anyone would believe her.

At the beginning of January 1994 Jackson's ex-chauffeur, Gary Hearne, made a statement, which was among court documents released by Jordan Chandler's lawyers. He revealed that he had driven the singer to the Chandler home in Los Angeles for twenty nights in a row during the four months when Jordan claimed that Jackson molested him. Hearne said that he bought a ruby necklace, ring and earrings worth £13,000 for Jordan's mother on Jackson's instructions. Other gifts for June included a video camera and recorder. Jordy got a £15,000 personal computer, and his father a watch. Hearne, questioned under oath by Jordan's lawyer, Larry Feldman, described the jewellery-buying expedition: 'He [Jackson] told me: "Pick something nice that has large stones." I asked him: "How much do you want to spend?" He said he didn't care.'

Also among the 480 pages of court documents were papers naming eight other boys wanted for questioning who, Jordan claimed, spent nights with Jackson.

Later there was some emotional testimony: in an eight-page statement filed in a Los Angeles court in February, Jackson's bodyguard Charlie Michals said: 'I saw Michael touching a young boy named Wade Robson in his crotch while apparently dancing with him. It was Mother's Day and I was told to take Joy Robson on a barn run to see all the animals on the estate. I took her in my truck and she was crying. She hadn't seen her son all day and she appeared nervous and concerned.'

After driving her to see the animals Michals took some food for Jackson and Wade. As she walked towards the dance studio, which had a mirrored wall in it, Michals claimed:

> I saw Michael Jackson draped over the front of Wade with his arms fully around the front and crotch of the little boy holding his hands and genitals and moving them up and down, while moving to the rhythm of the music that was playing. He was shouting 'Whee' repeatedly each time he pulled the boy's genitals up. I was stunned and shocked and withdrew. I didn't know what to do or what to say.

Jackson's sister LaToya had time and again punctured the myth of Michael's 'sainthood', but she saved her most damning attack for a press conference, which she called in December in Tel Aviv.

LaToya said she had decided to speak out because she could no longer stay silent about her brother's 'crimes' and wanted him to seek help:

> If I remain silent, then that means I feel the guilt and the humiliation that the children are feeling and I think it's very wrong. I cannot and will not be a silent collaborator of his crimes against small innocent children. Now you stop and think for one second and you tell me what thirty-five-year-old man is going to take a little boy and stay with him for thirty days and take another boy and stay with him for five days in a room and never leave the room?
>
> I have seen cheques payable to the parents of these children. I don't know if these children were

bought through the parents by Michael or not, but my mother showed me these cheques that Michael had written and the sums are very, very large amounts. I'm not speaking pennies. I love Michael very dearly but I feel even more sorry for these children because they don't have a life any more. These kids are going to be scarred for the rest of their life and I don't want to see any more innocent small children being affected in this way. It has always been little boys. I hope Michael gets help.

Just before Christmas 1993, LaToya once more attacked her brother. She appeared on Spanish television and commented:

Of course he'd say that, if the accusations were true he'd be finished. But I've got proof that it's all true and I'm here because it's got to stop. Young children's lives are being ruined and Michael needs urgent help. I love Michael. He's a wonderful loving, caring person. But I can't stand by and see small boys being abused.

Michael is a thirty-five-year-old man. A thirty-five-year-old man doesn't spend days locked in his bedroom with young boys. I've seen this going on. There's been masses of them. It's been going on for years. It has always been boys, never girls. Michael has never had a girlfriend in his life. I've tried to talk with him many times about it. He really needs help. I've warned him that if he didn't stop, that it would be public in the end. If Michael had been a regular person and not an idol this would have stopped long ago. He has to see a psychiatrist. Many of the boys he's known are now under psychiatric treatment, but it's my brother who needs it more than anyone.

LaToya also claimed that her mother had realized that Jackson was sleeping with little boys: 'She knows it and now she's denying it and that's what hurts. What hurts more than anything else is that if she knew that, why didn't she do something about it?' Katherine Jackson has always vehemently denied all these accusations.

Many people thought that LaToya's attacks on Michael – to whom she was once said to be very close – were purely motivated by jealousy. Her detractors point to the fact that her fame and the publicity that she gains for herself depend almost entirely on her brother and that for a decade she tried to launch a career as a top singer, releasing four albums, but with little success.

The rest of the Jackson clan dismissed her claims as nonsense. LaToya has been estranged from them ever since she agreed to pose for pictures in *Playboy* magazine in 1989. These pictures, which showed a nude LaToya caressing a snake, broke the last ties between her and her family.

A furious Katherine Jackson said in reply to LaToya's claims: 'LaToya is lying. And she knows it. I will tell her to her face that she is lying. It makes me sad that she is trying to sell Michael down the line.'

Jackson's brother Jermaine hit out at her too. It was Jermaine who, not long before, had himself attacked Michael. In a song he criticized Jackson for turning himself white through plastic surgery and 'skin-bleaching', and he was reported as saying that his brother could be guilty, though he later refuted this. But in December 1993 he stood loyally behind Michael and said of LaToya and her husband: 'They are just trying to jump on the bandwagon like everybody else. It's just a way of trying to make the family look bad.'

Joe Jackson also weighed in against his daughter and her husband: 'She lies all the time, this is how they make their money, by lying.' But Jack Gordon claimed that the family show of solidarity behind Michael was pure invention and maintained that the reason they were supporting him was because they were terrified of being cut off from his multi-million-pound fortune.

And so the allegations continued to flood in. Meanwhile Michael Jackson's health was still giving his friends and fans grave cause for concern. Elton John admitted recently that he was worried sick about his fellow star: 'He was fragile. I know for a fact that Jackson had a real problem with painkillers. It takes a while to get over that and he's gone right back into that mayhem situation over there. I fear for him.'

CHAPTER 7

The King of Pop

MANY PEOPLE – particularly those who had seen the astounding rise to fame of the Jackson Five in the seventies – could hardly believe that the Michael Jackson at the centre of the scandal that was shocking the world was the same Michael Jackson who was mesmerizing people with his singing, dancing and performing when he was five years old. At that age he was already – along with four of his brothers – a member of the group, which was formed by his domineering father, Joe. During the seventies the band scored hit after hit, including: 'I Want You Back', 'ABC', 'I'll Be There', 'Show You the Way to Go' and 'Shake Your Body', and it was always Michael who outshone all the other members. His fame, his fortune and his present bizarre circumstances were certainly a long way away from his humble beginnings in the poor steel town of Gary, Indiana.

Michael Jackson was born on 29 August 1958 to Joe and Katherine Jackson. He was the seventh child of nine. Most of his siblings – his five brothers, Jackie, Tito, Jermaine, Marlon and Randy, and three sisters, Janet, LaToya and Rebbie – have at one time or another shared the spotlight with him.

The Jackson family spent their early years in a most unlikely setting for a pop dynasty. Gary in the fifties and sixties was a poor, rough and heavily industrial town with high unemployment. The work that there was was back-breaking and involved long hours. Joe Jackson worked an eight-hour shift as a crane-operator at Inland Steel in East Chicago. He often kept the family above the bread line by supplementing his regular job through part-time welding work.

The Jacksons' home was a modest two-bedroom affair that had been bought in 1950 for just over £5,500. It was a tight squeeze to get eleven people into it, but somehow they managed. Katherine and Joe shared one bedroom, the boys shared another, and the girls slept on a converted sofa-bed. Michael once said of the house: 'You could take five steps from the front door and you'd be out the back.'

The Jackson family had to learn to do without and were taught strict family and religious values. It was a harsh upbringing for Michael and his brothers and sisters. Their mother was a Jehovah's Witness. Members of this strange faith are forbidden to give or receive blood even in life or death emergencies. Though Katherine, who walked with a limp after a childhood bout of polio, could not get her husband to share in her religious beliefs, he was happy for their children to have the teaching of the Witnesses instilled in them because the rules of the church were rigid and stern and Joe himself was a tough disciplinarian. If he caught his children misbehaving, Joe would not hesitate to discipline them, and both Michael and LaToya spoke out later about the beatings to which their father subjected them.

Joe Jackson also brought in much-needed extra dollars through his music. He played the guitar in a five-piece rhythm and blues band called the Falcons in the neigh-bourhood clubs and bars. This guitar was the starting note for the Jackson Five. When Joe went out to work, Tito would sneak up to his father's bedroom and try to play it. His brothers Jermaine (who was only six) and Jackie (nine

– the eldest) would learn songs and sing along to Tito's playing. But their secret music sessions were discovered when Tito broke one of the guitar strings. Joe flew into a fury. Tito pleaded with him that he and his brothers weren't goofing around but were making music. When they insisted on showing him what they had learnt an incredulous Joe was startled by their skills. And so it was that the talent of the Jacksons was first uncovered.

Joe rehearsed the three boys for three hours every day; Marlon and Michael would watch and learn. Joe was later to admit: 'When the other kids would be out on the street playing games, my boys were in the house working – trying to learn how to be something in life.'

To begin with the three brothers were joined by two cousins and the group was called the Jackson Family – Michael was not in the group's original line-up because he was too young. Then Michael and Marlon took their places and the band was renamed the Jackson Five. It was immediately obvious what a musical prodigy young Michael was. He had a voice that could take your breath away and a wonderful gift for mimicry that enabled him to imitate songs and dances perfectly. It was decided that Michael should replace Jermaine as the lead singer. Jermaine recalled: 'He became this great little imitator. He'd see something – another kid dance, or maybe James Brown on TV – and the next thing you knew, Michael has it memorized and knew what to do with it. He loved to dance too. You'd always catch him dancing for himself in the mirror. He'd go off alone and practise and then come back and show us this new step.'

The boys started on their ascent up the pop ladder through local talent contests. The first one they entered took place at a high school in their neighbourhood – Roosevelt High – and Michael stole the show. The group were singing the Temptations' slinkily seductive 'My Girl' when, during a musical break in the middle of this song, they suddenly launched into the Robert Parker dance classic, 'Barefootin''. Five-year-old Michael captivated the whole audience by kicking off his shoes and dancing barefoot right across the stage. The crowd went wild and the group picked up the first prize. Michael remembered: 'After that we started winning every talent show we entered. The whole house was full of trophies, and my father was so proud. So proud, I can't tell you. Probably the happiest I ever saw my mother and father was back there in Gary when we were winning those talent shows. That's when we were closest. Back in the beginning when we didn't have anything but our talent.'

Talent contests would take the boys as far as Chicago, Cleveland, Washington, DC, Boston and Philadelphia. It was gruelling, punishing work. The boys would be driven to the club venues by their father and then return home in the early hours of the morning. They'd go straight to bed, snatch a few hours' sleep and then get up for school the next morning.

In August 1967 they had their first taste of real stardom when they played at New York's world-famous Harlem Apollo theatre. Here they won the amateur contest. In J. Randy Taraborrelli's fascinating biography, *The Magic and the Madness*, Jackson recalled the excitement of it all. He was stunned by the reaction from the crowd: 'At the Apollo, girls bought stuff for us. You know, watches, and rings and things. And we didn't even tell them to do it. We didn't even know they were coming. I mean, we didn't even know them and they were giving us watches.'

Eventually the Jacksons decided that if they wanted true pop success they had to leave Gary. For a year Jackson's parents were separated as Joe took the boys to Los Angeles while a heart-broken Katherine stayed at home. Two years later, in October 1969, the Jackson Five were signed up by one of the most successful record labels in the world – Motown, whose huge hit roster included Stevie Wonder, Smokey Robinson and Diana Ross.

Diana Ross was involved in some myth-making hype when the Jacksons were signed up: it was claimed that the former Supreme beauty had discovered the band at a concert in Gary in 1967 and had raved about them to Motown's shrewd boss, Berry Gordy, who was also Diana's lover at the time. It wasn't true, but it was a great publicity stunt and everyone ran with it. Gordy arranged for the boys and their father to stay in a rather down-at-heel hotel across from the Hollywood studios where they recorded their material. But the Jackson family didn't mind – they were in Los Angeles now and everything looked rosy.

Motown were busting with confidence over their new signings. Michael remembers Gordy telling them right from the outset: 'I'm going to make you kids the biggest thing in the world. You are going to have hit after hit. You are going to be in the history books. So get ready.'

Gordy was to be as good as his word but he didn't want to leave anything to chance so he once again drafted in Diana Ross to help out. She threw a party to which she invited the big wheels of the music industry and the press. The invite read: 'Please join me in welcoming a brilliant musical group at the North Rodeo Drive, Beverly Hills. The Jackson Five, featuring sensational eight-year-old Michael Jackson, will perform live at the party. (signed) Diana Ross.'

It didn't matter that Michael Jackson was really ten years old any more than it mattered that Diana Ross hadn't really discovered the Jackson Five. It was a great piece of hype and from that day on Jackson was to be painfully aware of the power of good, old-fashioned public relations. He later admitted: 'I figured out at an early age that if someone said something about me that wasn't true, it was a lie. But if someone said something about my image that wasn't true, then it was okay. Because then it wasn't a lie, it was public relations.'

While his brothers and father shuffled between hotel and motel, Michael, because he was so young and because Gordy believed he was so special, was given a homely, stable environment – living with Diana Ross. Gordy admitted: 'It was a calculated thing. I wanted him to be around her. People think it was an accident that he stayed there. It wasn't. I wanted Diana to teach him whatever she could.'

If she had been intended as a mother-substitute for Jackson, the idea backfired. Instead, Jackson, who missed his mother terribly, developed a crush on Diana – a crush that persisted for years. But much more significant were her life-style and her charisma. She became a role model for the young boy. 'I'm going to be just like her when I grow up,' he would say to himself.

In October 1969 'I Want You Back' was released; it was the Jackson Five's first single on Motown and there was no stopping them. After ten weeks this delicious upbeat slice of dance, featuring Michael's sweet, urgent, pleading falsetto, was the number one record in America, toppling a song from the film *Butch Cassidy and the Sundance Kid*, 'Raindrops Keep Falling on My Head'. It sold over two million copies in the Jacksons' homeland and a further four million in the rest of the world, and soared to the number two slot in Britain. On 18 October 1969, a few days after the release of their debut single, the group made their first appearance on national TV. 'The Hollywood Palace' was hosted by Diana Ross. They stole the show and the young Michael Jackson even managed to upstage legendary entertainer Sammy Davis Jnr.

At the end of that year the Jackson Five's first album, *Diana Ross Presents the Jackson Five*, was released. It sold an amazing 600,000 copies in America alone. Success after success followed. In February 1970 the second Jackson single, 'ABC', in the same vein as 'I Want You Back' but even more inventive, came out. This, too, went to the top of the American charts, sold over two million copies and kicked the Beatles' 'Let It Be' off the number one slot. In Britain it crashed into the top ten, reaching number eight.

The group's next single release was 'The Love You Save' which once again ousted the Beatles, the most popular band in the history of pop, from their place at the top of the US charts, which they had held with 'The Long and Winding Road', while in Britain it soared to the number seven position. After just three releases the Jackson Five were in the record books themselves as the first group ever to have their first three records all hit the number one spot.

A succession of hits followed: 'I'll Be There', 'Mama's Pearl', 'Lookin' Through the Windows' and 'Doctor My Eyes'. Their fourth single, 'I'll Be There' (which reached number four in the British charts), just failed to make the top slot in America. It was kept off the number one position by the Osmonds, another teen pin-up group, who were seen as the Jackson Five's biggest rivals and who kept up an energetic battle against them – a battle which only served to increase each band's popularity.

As the Jacksons' hits kept on coming, Michael Jackson became the idol of the group and the centre of worldwide teen mania. The Jackson Five's every gig was mobbed by thousands of lovesick, screaming admirers, hurling presents and love-letters at them. It was mayhem and, for their youngest member, a portent of what was to come. At one show in Philadelphia the band were mobbed by 3,500 frantic girls. There were not enough security guards to cope and extra police had to be drafted in so that the brothers could escape from the stadium. Michael, whose sweet, happy, innocent looks had made him the band's number one pin-up, was petrified and in tears when he finally made it back to his hotel room. Jermaine recalled:

'Michael was scared to death. The rest of us were more amazed than scared, but he was genuinely frightened.'

It was not long before the obvious happened: Michael Jackson began releasing solo records. His first, released in February 1972, was the haunting ballad 'Got to Be There', which reached number four in the American charts and number five in Britain. He followed this up three months later with 'Rockin' Robin', an upbeat noveltyesque song from the fifties about a dancing robin redbreast. This hit number two in America and number three in Britain. Other solo hits followed, including 'Ain't No Sunshine' and 'Ben', a song from the movie of the same name about a boy in love with a pet rat. At this point it became evident that Jackson was a star in his own right. He was not to leave his brothers for another seven years – 1979 – but it was an inevitability just waiting to happen.

But Michael was not the first to leave the Jackson Five: the first escapee was Jermaine. In 1973 Jermaine married Motown boss Berry Gordy's daughter Hazel, and so fused two powerful show-business dynasties. Their marriage, however, began to interfere with the Jackson family's business affairs and eventually, in 1975, Jermaine left the clan. In doing so he was seen as siding with his wife and Berry Gordy, and rejecting his immediate family. Before he left the Jacksons had pulled off what was, for a black band, a great coup: they played Las Vegas and immediately broadened their appeal immeasurably.

As Michael Jackson entered his late teens, two important things happened to the singer, who was by now quite clued up about the machinations of the pop industry. Firstly, his voice started to break, and secondly, he became unhappy with the music the Jacksons were playing. Recording was no longer a family group effort; now Michael would have to lay down his lead part of the record first, and then the brothers would add to it at a later date. The crunch came when the seventeen-year-old Michael arranged a secret meeting with Berry Gordy about his and his brothers' future. He wasn't happy about the way his father was managing the group, he wasn't happy about the money the band were earning, and he wasn't happy about Motown's financial investment in the group. It was reported that Michael had said he was not prepared to put up with this treatment. Joe Jackson hit the roof when he found out that Michael had gone behind his back to see Berry Gordy, and Michael's brothers were furious, too.

Yet that meeting was a turning point for the group. Unable to renegotiate contracts and get a better deal, Joe Jackson decided not to renew his sons' contracts with Motown Records. Instead, in late 1975, negotiations began to move with Epic Records – owned by the mighty CBS recording giant. All the brothers signed the contract apart from Jermaine, who stood by his wife and Berry Gordy. Jermaine was now replaced by the family's youngest son, Randy, and from now on the band were called the Jacksons instead of the Jackson Five.

But the ties between Michael Jackson and Berry Gordy were not completely severed. The two teamed up again when Michael made his first movie, *The Wiz*, a black version of the children's classic fantasy tale, *The Wizard of Oz*. He starred alongside Diana Ross and played the scarecrow. This role called for him to don a heavy disguise, which he enjoyed enormously. The film came out in 1978, costing £24 million, and although Michael got good reviews it was a major flop.

Michael went back to recording with the Jacksons, making the album *Destiny*, which encapsulated the disco feel of the time. It included such classic dance-floor fillers as 'Blame It on the Boogie', and also 'Shake Your Body (Down to the Ground)', a track written by Michael and his brother Randy. But in the course of the tour that followed, Michael complained that he was feeling tired and losing

his voice. Eventually something had to give, and it proved
to be his career with the Jackson family.

Part of Jackson's Epic deal was that he would be allowed to
release solo albums. The first one proved to be an immediate
worldwide success and after that there was no looking back.
The album, *Off the Wall*, was produced by Quincy Jones and
was released in August 1979. The LP showed an incredible
maturity, and was packed with some spectacular songs,
including the breakneck 'Don't Stop Till You Get Enough',
the tear-jerking ballad, 'She's Out of My Life', and such
great tunes as 'Rock With You', 'Working Day and Night',
and 'Get On the Floor', and of course the title track.

   The album launched a parade of hit singles – a pattern
that was to become familiar to Jackson fans. The first two
album tracks both reached number three in the UK charts,
while 'Off the Wall' got to number seven. Also featured
was 'Girlfriend', a song about a man stealing a girl from
her current boyfriend after a clandestine affair, written by
Paul McCartney – the first collaboration between the two
stars in song. The album sold a staggering eight million
copies worldwide, including one million copies in Britain.

   Michael Jackson seemed to be everywhere now. To cash
in on the singer's new-found meteoric superstardom, his
old record company Motown released his beautiful,
passionate ballad 'One Day In Your Life', which rocketed
to the top spot. There was more work ahead for Jackson
as he rejoined his brothers for their *Triumph* tour to promote the group's album of the same name.

   The singer was becoming ever more ambitious, ever
more conscious of his career, and he wanted much more
control of it. To this end he sacked his father from managing his affairs which caused a bitter dispute between them.
Later, in his autobiography, *Moonwalk*, Michael told of his
relationship with his father: 'My father looked out for
both our interests and his . . . but I still don't know him,

and that's sad, for a son who hungers to know his father.'

Michael followed up *Off the Wall* with a monster of an album. *Thriller*, released in December 1982, became the biggest-selling record of all time – at the time of writing it has sold an astonishing 47 million copies. It was a painstakingly-made album: the singer spent almost three years on its creation. Ever the perfectionist, Jackson cut and re-cut tracks again and again until he was happy with the product. *Thriller* was an ambition he had nurtured since childhood. As he revealed in *Moonwalk*: 'Ever since I was a little boy, I had dreamed of creating the biggest record of all time.'

Among the riveting tracks on the album was 'Billie Jean', in which the singer tells how a girl has accused him of fathering her child. It was a plaintive, passionate, breathless drama – one of the best songs that has ever been recorded. The video which accompanied it had as its centrepiece Jackson's mesmerizing dancing, including his famous 'moonwalking' steps – a magical effect whereby it appears the floor underneath his feet is moving backwards like an escalator in reverse. The song and the video made such an irresistible combination that the powerful MTV pop video channel, previously averse to showing 'black video', made 'Billie Jean' a first: the sales of the album rocketed and a slice of pop history was created.

The video for the album's title track was also a landmark. It blended horror with pop and was the longest and most expensive video ever made. In it Jackson is physically transformed before the viewer's eyes from a twinkle-toed adolescent into a gruesome werewolf. The video was directed by top Hollywood director John Landis, who was also responsible for *An American Werewolf in London*, and featured a cameo appearance by the late horror movie veteran Vincent Price. Again the video was interspersed with some fabulous dancing.

The album also featured such great tracks as the pulsating 'Wanna Be Startin' Something', the sweet 'PYT (Pretty

Young Thing)', and the wonderfully wistful 'Human Nature'. It also included Jackson's duet with Paul McCartney, 'The Girl Is Mine', a smoochy number about two men battling for the love of the same girl.

Jackson followed up *Thriller* with *Bad*, in September 1987. The album and the image were altogether more aggressively sexual, with Jackson posing moodily on the album's cover, clothed in black leather jacket and trousers complete with chains and studs. Though it could not match *Thriller*'s record figures, it was again a resounding success – achieving the kind of sales most artists don't even reach when *all* their album sales are added together: it notched up around 27 million. Again, videos were crucial to the album and no expense or energy was spared in making them. The video for the single 'Bad' was made by the gritty, tough Hollywood director Martin Scorcese, famous for his shockingly brutal films, including *Taxi Driver*, and it featured the singer dancing and fighting with a tough street gang in the New York subway.

The album once again comprised a seamless blending of up-tempo tracks and mellow ballads. 'Smooth Criminal', an up-tempo track which reached number eight in the UK, based its video on the gangster years of prohibition in America, and featured an amazing dance track in which the star and his dancers seem to defy gravity. In 'The Way You Make Me Feel', another up-tempo hit, the singer is attempting to chat up a girl, who is oblivious to his advances. Jackson's duet partner on this album was a beautiful young singer-songwriter called Seidah Garrett, who sang with him the romantic 'I Just Can't Stop Loving You', which soared to number one on both sides of the Atlantic and gave the singer his third solo number one in Britain and his fifth in America.

The 1988 tour which came off the back of the album – and which was sponsored by Pepsi-Cola – was a magnificent success and confirmed Jackson's reputation as the

world's greatest showman. It was a show crammed to overflowing with hits, nostalgia and wonderful special effects.
I flew to Tokyo to catch the opening date and I loved it.

If Jackson's fans thought his songs were works of magic,
so too did the singer. He described the way in which his
hit tunes came to him as something mystical, something
God-given.

> It's something you are born with. I am inspired by
> things around me and I like creating magic – there
> is nothing like it. I try to do it with everything I do.
> I have always said I don't write my songs – I am just
> a source, a tunnel. I feel like my songs have been up
> in space and have been written before. It is a higher
> force, making it happen. All my songs – like 'Billie
> Jean' and 'Beat It' – have been written before and
> then they come to me.

After *Bad* came *Dangerous*, and once again Jackson talked
about the album in mystical, religious utterances. He
claimed that he wasn't just a singer, but a messenger from
God sent to earth to share with the world his gift of divine
music and dance. He compared himself with such geniuses
as Mozart and Tchaikovsky and said that the world would
be listening to his music a hundred years from now. In an
interview with *Ebony* magazine he said:

> I really believe that God has chosen me in the same
> way that Michelangelo, Leonardo da Vinci, Mozart,
> Mohammed Ali and Martin Luther King were chosen.
> I don't like taking credit for my songs because they
> come from God. I'm just the instrument through
> which the music flows. Deep inside I feel the world we
> live in is a huge monumental symphonic orchestra. In
> its most basic form all of creation is sound – and music.

Of *Dangerous* he said: 'I wanted to do an album like Tchaikovsky's Nutcracker Suite, so that in a thousand years from

now people would still be listening to it. I would like to see people of all races, hundreds of years from now, pulling out songs from the album and dissecting it.'

The hype during the weeks leading up to the album's release in November 1991 was unrelenting, but the singer was determined that his first album for four years, an album that had been long awaited by his army of fans, should be a huge success. By the time it came out there couldn't have been many people among the record-buying public of the world who didn't know about it. The album had been a long time coming and was much altered since the singer began recording it. The ever perfectionist Jackson changed his mind constantly about the kind of album he wanted and the songs he wanted on it. Initial release dates were missed as the singer added more and more songs to the album, and when it finally came out the singer presented the world with a double album which was crammed full of seventy-seven minutes' worth of music.

Dangerous was different from Jackson's previous albums. It wasn't just that the singer no longer had the trusted and inventive producer Quincy Jones at the helm – this LP had a triumvirate of captains in charge of production: Bill Bottrell, Bruce Swedien and Terry Riley, a vibrant twenty-five-year-old who had come up with the punchy new jack-swing sound of Bobby Brown, and who co-wrote seven of the album's cuts. No, it was that where other Michael Jackson albums led and became landmarks in pop, this one borrowed heavily from the current fashionable sounds around. On some of the album's cuts it was as if Jackson had stopped trusting his own inventiveness and magical intuition and had decided to follow musical trends – hence the inclusion of rap and the disjointed feel about much of the album.

Still, there were many good songs in there, among them 'Black or White', the foot-stomping 'Jam', which opened the album, and the passionate 'In the Closet'. It also included reminders of Jackson's greatness with such songs as the emotional ballad, 'Will You Be There?', the hypnotic 'Remember the Time', and the rather sentimental anthem, 'Heal the World'. That song became one of the highlights of the *Dangerous* tour, with its references to the suffering of children all over the world. Another sentimental song on the album was 'Gone Too Soon', which was dedicated to the memory of little Ryan White, the American boy who died of AIDS which he contracted through a blood transfusion.

The first single from the album, 'Black or White', a delicious blend of funk and rock, was released amid much hullabaloo. It was accompanied by a video – a kaleidoscope of fast-moving images lasting eleven minutes which cost a staggering £3.5 million to make. It was slammed by many critics as being flashy, indulgent and a waste of money. The video opens with a portrayal of a suburban American family home: Macaulay Culkin (Jackson's child-star friend) angers his dad, played by 'Cheers' star George Wendt, with his loud guitar-playing. It then moves on to feature Michael Jackson dancing, first with cowboys and Indians in a Wild West sequence, then with a traditionally dressed Asian dancer, and then, in a snowstorm scene, with Russian Cossacks. One of the highlights of the video is an amazing technique called 'morphing', which allows the faces of different races and sexes to transform one into the other. Another highlight is Jackson's spectacular change from a wild black panther into a manic angry man during a scene in which the singer violently smashes up a car. The sequence was eventually chopped after protests from people who said it was too violent and sexual. But the image had worked because the resulting controversy ensured headlines for Jackson all over the world.

On the heels of the *Dangerous* album, of course, came the tour which would prove to be such a disaster for Michael Jackson.

CHAPTER 8

Childhood Reclaimed

As MICHAEL JACKSON'S FAME GREW, he became increasingly strange. His bizarreness was basically a combination of three things: a show-business life which had detached him totally from the real world, an incredible sensitivity and shyness, and a shrewd understanding that hype could propel him into the rarefied realms of myth.

And the stories about his behaviour grew stranger by the moment, filling pages and pages of tabloid copy — stories claiming that he slept in an oxygen chamber and that he bathed in bottled mineral water. When he shopped, he did not just shop for the Rolls-Royces, or for the jewellery and haute couture fashion items that most stars went for but instead sought out such things as the remains of the 'Elephant Man', a Victorian freak called John Merrick, with whom he closely identified. So fascinated was Jackson by the Elephant Man that he bid a rumoured $2 million to buy his remains from a London hospital. His home also had other mummified remains in it.

Some of Jackson's eccentricities were revealed by the star's former employees Mark and Faye Quindoy. One day they discovered the singer sitting on the floor, tearing up £50,000 worth of thousand dollar bills and throwing them up into the air like confetti. As the Quindoys looked on, astonished, the star giggled and said that the shredded dollars looked pretty and that it was only money. The star had apparently told them that he spent £150,000 a year on new bulbs and flowers for his spectacular gardens and that he cried whenever flowers died. They also said that Jackson would only eat food if it was named after Disney characters: his eating regime consisted of such meals as a Goofy salad, Pluto pie and Minnie Mouse milk shakes.

These are some of the tales that were spun about Michael Jackson. It is hard to separate the fact from the fiction, if indeed there is any fiction. Because if these kind of tales were made up, then Jackson not only turned a blind eye to them but often invented them himself because he loved the idea of these modern-day pop fables. He felt that the strange, eccentric persona that had grown up around him added to his status and made him the most talked-about show-business star on the planet. And that was the way he liked it.

The confusion about what was real and what was not is best illustrated by the legend of the oxygen chamber. When Jackson appeared on the Oprah Winfrey show in February 1993 he dismissed the story as a complete fabrication. This was part of his quest at the time to present himself to the world as a normal person: after a decade of being the focus for eccentric stories, he felt they were getting out of hand and might even be damaging his career. His *Dangerous* album had not sold as well as expected and his tour had received a number of lukewarm reviews. Yet the tales of his oxygen tent cannot be dismissed as the complete fiction that he said they were. The stunt had been dreamed up by Jackson and his manager, Frank Dileo, to gain publicity for the 1988 *Bad* tour. Jackson had apparently become fascinated with the hyperbaric oxygen chamber he saw on a visit to a hospital burns unit. He was obsessed by longevity, and believed that by using this chamber he could live to be 150 years old. Janet Jackson once admitted that her brother had constant dark brooding thoughts about dying and that was why he indulged in his mania for health foods and for weird contraptions like his oxygen chamber. Janet revealed:

> Michael has always had a thing about death ever since he was a kid. It has dominated his thinking. It got worse when he turned thirty. I remember when that happened I tried to cheer him up by saying to him that life really began at thirty, but he wouldn't have any of it. He looked me in the eye and told me: 'Janet, we all start to die the minute we are born.'
>
> That is why Michael has such a strict health regime and why he uses the oxygen chamber. He believes that things like that will help keep him alive a long time. He feels he has so much to offer the world and is petrified of it all coming to an end.

So Jackson himself cannot be blameless for the stories that have been exploding around him. And many of these stories were true – the singer *did* have his picture taken with his chimpanzee Bubbles, whom he dressed in children's clothes; he *did* pose lovingly with his snake Crusher; and he *did* go out on huge shopping expeditions to toy shops all over the world.

Jackson's strangeness was coupled by an amazing transformation in his looks. His desire to be different is there for everyone to see in his face: he has changed it out of all recognition through a series of plastic surgery operations and even, it is said, by bleaching his skin (though recently he blamed his pale skin on a terrible skin disease called vitiligo). The surgery has given his once chubby African features – the broad nose and full lips – a Caucasian and feminine appearance. Many people think that his face now looks grotesque and unnatural: it is a face on which gender, race and age have been blurred. Jackson's appearance on the Oprah Winfrey show was also aimed at defending himself against reports that plastic surgery had made him look 'monstrous' – as I had claimed in a piece I wrote for the *Daily Mirror* – which had upset the sensitive star. His sister LaToya had challenged his claim that he had had only minimal plastic surgery.

Some say that Jackson's obsession with plastic surgery has its roots in his childhood – a childhood he spent hating his large nose and even being taunted with the nickname 'Big Nose'. Acne eruptions also wrecked much of his teenage life: the acne was so severe that Jackson was devastated by his appearance: 'I seemed to have a pimple for every oil gland. I became subconsciously scarred by this. I got very shy and became embarrassed to meet people. The effect on me was that it messed up my whole personality.'

Others say that he changed his features because he wanted to look as little as possible like the father he was said to despise and who caused him such hurt during his childhood.

These are plausible arguments but they do not really explain why he changed his face so drastically. All-important is Jackson's desire to be special, to be different – no matter what it takes – and to create something that the world has never seen. It is a desire which is shaped out of courage and even madness, but it is a desire that Jackson has achieved.

Some psychiatrists, however, have speculated along more sinister lines: that the plastic surgery could be seen as self-mutilation; while others say that it is possibly because the singer was sexually molested as a boy. Perhaps his extensive plastic surgery has made it hard for Jackson to have relationships with people of his own age; they could not fail to bring up the subject of his strange looks. Children, even if they found his appearance strange, would not be shocked by it and would merely see it as one more manifestation of the Jackson magic.

Jackson's strange appearance was matched by his

strange behaviour. He hardly ever spoke in public and when he did so, it was in a high-pitched whisper. But could there be more to the bizarre behaviour than just a desire to become the stuff that show-business legends are made of? (After all, the last thing we want is for our stars to be ordinary.) Could it not be that Jackson's oddness gave him a shield behind which he could lead a private life without suffering intrusion — a shield that kept his private life shrouded in secrecy. And Jackson treasured this secrecy: 'I'm just like a haemophiliac,' he once said. 'I can't afford to be scratched in any way.'

Behind this foil he could engage in any kind of behaviour he wanted, knowing that it could be passed off as just another of his eccentricities. Behind this foil he also cut some of the biggest money-spinning deals that the show-business world has ever seen. His eccentricity and his childlike nature should not be confused with simplicity or buffoonery, for his retinue of aides, his family, and his friends will all testify that he is intelligent, businesslike and quick-witted. They paint an entirely different picture of Michael Jackson to the one his public sees — an image likened to the pop offspring of Peter Pan and ET.

Legendary producer Quincy Jones, who produced Jackson's first three solo albums, told me that all the rumours of Jackson's eccentricity and weirdness belie his other side — a side that most fans never see:

Michael is overwhelmingly sane, despite all the odd-ball rumours flying around. He's far from crazy — and I should know. I've been around him for a long time. He's one of the smartest and most together people I've met. He knows exactly what he wants and goes for it. To outsiders, his life-style may seem unreal but then it's been shaped by the fact that he's been in the business since he was five years old. I've worked with some crazy people in my time, but Michael isn't one of them. So many people go nuts after just one hit, either because of drugs or pressure. But Michael's had hit after hit and stayed quite sane. He never ever tries to act like a big superstar. He's a very modest guy who never throws his weight around. He's polite, patient and calm. When he turns the lights off in the recording studio or hides behind a couch, that's only because he's incredibly shy. He hates boasting about his talent.

Jones believes that Jackson's star sign gives him the sanity to balance his eccentricities:

Michael's a Virgo and Virgos have it all together. He thinks in a very meticulous way and pays great attention to detail. He knows all about what is going on in the world. One of the problems he's concerned about is the way young people are being ruined by drugs. He feels music can give a positive message to the world and that's what he's doing . . . I believe Michael will become the Sinatra of his generation. He'll still be singing when he's seventy.

Michael Jackson doesn't much relish the company of adults. Of course, he can get along with them – if he couldn't, he wouldn't have been able to cut the merciless money-spinning deals that have made his career so amazingly profitable. But if Jackson had his choice he would rather spend his time with animals and children. And, for the last decade, that is exactly what he has done. His Neverland home boasts a huge zoo overflowing with animals, including elephants, llamas, giraffes, snakes and monkeys. For a long time one of his closest friends was the chimpanzee called Bubbles who travelled everywhere with him and even slept in his bedroom. He dressed the monkey in miniature versions of his own clothes, held hands with it,

and was even said to be learning how to speak 'chimpanzee' so that they could communicate. Reports claimed that
he once bought Bubbles a £40,000 antique clock.

The other friends he hung out with included a llama
called Louis, a sheep called Mr Tibbs, and a 300-lb boa
constrictor called Crusher.

When Jackson was on tour in Singapore he allowed
himself to forget his troubles by indulging in some
behaviour that was close to his heart – he went animal
crackers and romped with a sextet of orang-utans. The
singer asked Singapore's zoological gardens to close for the
day so that he could visit it in private. Though officials
couldn't honour his request, they did the next best thing:
they sent six orang-utans to Jackson's hotel. Jackson
played with them as he sat with Liz Taylor by the hotel's
beautiful swimming pool and was so pleased by the apes'
antics that he even hugged and kissed one of the animals.

Bernard Harrison, the zoo's executive director, said:
'The orang-utans were made up of two adults, two youngsters and two babies. Mr Jackson was absolutely riveted
by them. He hardly took his eyes off them as they played.'

At first the singer wanted to entertain his ape pals in
his hotel suite. But the hotel managers said that they could
wreak havoc, so it was decided to hold the strange tea-
party outside. It was quite a tea-party: a white-gloved
butler served drinks to Jackson, Taylor and Larry Fortenski
as they sat on the marble terrace beside the pool. The apes
sat at two marble-topped tables, where they slurped cola
out of bottles. They were no ordinary monkeys: one of the
orang-utans, Ah-Ming, was the country's unofficial mascot
and appeared on stamps and regularly met VIPs.

After the party finished zoo officials, seeing how much
the singer had enjoyed himself, invited Jackson along for
an after-hours visit to the zoo. He and Liz Taylor were
driven around the seventy-acre site in a van. Bernard
Harrison, described how: 'Mr Jackson was awed by what

he saw there. He loved watching one of the elephants perform a trick with a hoop, spinning it around its trunk. When we got to the crocodile area he was completely riveted. One of the crocodiles was over five metres long and Mr Jackson was mesmerized. When he saw a mandrill with its bright colours he jumped out of the van and stood looking at it completely transfixed.'

But Jackson's real fondness is for children. They are his true soul-mates. Psychiatrists have speculated that this could be because, having been a star since the age of five, he never had a proper childhood himself; now, by associat-ing with children, he is able to reinvent that lost childhood. He told Oprah Winfrey in a fascinating show in February 1993 (his first TV interview for fourteen years):

Because I was a child star, I didn't get to do the things that other children take for granted, like having friends, slumber parties or just hanging out. People wonder why I always have children round. That is because I can find the thing that I never had through them. When I was little it was always work, work, work. I relate much better to children than I do to adults. I find them easier to talk to. I find them more fun to be with. One of the reasons I have them around is that I just want to be loved.

At Jackson's home he has a collection of mannequins to whom he often talks in moments of loneliness. He once said of his love for mannequins: 'I guess I want to bring them to life. I like to imagine talking to them. I think I'm accompanying myself with friends because being an entertainer you just can't tell who is your friend. And I know the mannequins can be my friends. I love talking to them.' He also said that part of his loneliness stems from that stolen childhood, a theme that runs through many of his thoughts and words. The fantasy world – a retreat during his teens, when he often felt like a caged animal – was created because 'I was lonely. I used to cry from loneliness. I would look out and see all the children playing and it would make me cry.'

My brothers and sisters also missed out on a lot that most other kids take for granted. I think that one of the reasons I often shut myself away is because of my childhood. One of my favourite pastimes is being with children – talking with them and playing with them. They revive me because they help me find my own inner child without whom I would be lost. I love being with children. They don't have any of the bad points that adults have like lying and scheming. If I was allowed one wish it would be that all the children all over the world find happiness. There is too much misery and war on earth. I would love to see world peace in my lifetime. So far I've been lucky because all my dreams have come true. I hope this does too.

Jackson himself once told me in a very revealing interview he gave when he was in London:

I love children so much. Sometimes I think I would like to get married, but I know I can't because I have so many things to do. But I would love to have kids, I'd like to have twenty. I'd like to adopt them, I really would. They're everything I wish the world would be – they don't know any prejudice, they're not phoney and if they don't like you, they'll tell you. Grown-ups pretend they like you when deep down inside they hate you. When I'm upset about a recording session, I'll dash off to the school yard just to be around them.

Producer Quincy Jones told me of the magical effect that Jackson has on children:

> Children love Michael as much as he loves them. My kids are ecstatic when he's around. They can't wait to see him. A lot of adults find it hard to communicate with kids, but not Michael. He has a gift for it. Michael loves animals for the same reasons he loves children because unlike adults they don't have any falseness about them. He trusts them. And he is one hundred per cent right.

Michael's older brother Jermaine, who at one time was the sibling he was closest to, also told me about Jackson's fascination for children:

> Michael is in many ways a kid in a grown-up person's body. I think a lot of that has to do with the fact that he did not really have a normal childhood because right from the time he was just a few years old he has always been on stage performing . . . He did miss out on childhood and all the things that go with it and he is making up for it now. He is in a position where he can indulge his every whim, and I do not see that there is anything harmful in that. That is why Michael loves to surround himself with children so much. None of us really had too much chance to play and do all the things that kids do when they are growing up. So that is what he is doing now. I do not think there is anything dangerous in that. If more of us stayed as childlike as he is, the world would be a better place. When children get together there is lots of love and happiness, but when a group of adults do there is arguing and fighting.

These beliefs have been reiterated by Michael Jackson on numerous occasions. In his autobiography, *Moonwalk*, he admits: 'I love being around kids. They aren't jaded. They get excited by things we've forgotten to get excited about any more.' 'What I love about kids,' he has said, 'is that they notice everything. They love the world. They're not cynical at all – they're so natural, so unself-concious.'

Jackson himself identifies strongly with Peter Pan, the boy who never grew up, and named his palatial home Neverland; he has read and reread the book whose opening line declares: 'Every child grows up but one.' So Jackson created a magic kingdom for himself where he could live as a modern-day Peter Pan surrounded by animals, circus rides and young children.

Another strong belief of Michael Jackson's is that it is children who hold the key to the future of the world. That is why he has lavished so much affection on them: 'I realize that many of our world's problems today, from inner-city crime to large-scale war and terrorism, are a result that children have had their childhoods stolen from them. The magic, the mystery and the innocence of a child's heart are the seeds of creativity that will heal the world.'

Certainly his love for children is no empty boast. He regularly opens up his magnificent home to deprived and terminally ill children. There, in his arcade of games and on the magical funfair rides, they can forget their ills for a while. He has donated millions to helping children – and has founded a charity, Heal the World, to achieve that end.

Jackson decided to make children and his love of children the theme running through his whole *Dangerous* tour. On 23 June 1992 around noon he launched the tour – his first for four years – in a private aircraft hangar at London's Heathrow airport. On stage with Michael were children from ten countries – including the UK, Germany, Spain, Italy and France. Each of them told about the issues that most affected them and the young people in their countries. It was a moving and emotional scenario – I was one of the journalists there.

After the children had spoken Jackson himself gave a short speech:

> Our children are the most beautiful, most sweet, most treasured of our creations. And yet, every minute at least twenty-eight children die. Today our children are at risk of being killed by diseases and by the violence of war, guns, abuse, and neglect. Children have few rights and no one to speak for them. They have no voice in our world. God and nature has blessed me with a voice. Now I want to use it to help children speak for themselves. I have founded the Heal the World Foundation to be the voice of the voiceless: the children. Please, join with me and the children to help heal the world. Together, parents, communities, governments – all people of the world – we must put our children first. Finally and most importantly, I want to tell the children of the world: You are all our children, each one of you is my child, and I love you.

At its launch conference the Heal the World Foundation's mission was also made clear by the organizers: to heal the world by helping children everywhere. They pin-pointed three goals: firstly to make the safety, health, and development of children the world's highest priority; secondly to be the voice of the voiceless by focusing worldwide attention on the needs and rights of all children and by providing children with a forum to express their unique vision for healing the world; and thirdly to help to create a world where children will live without violence, where children will be free of disease and have healthy lives, and where each generation will have the opportunity to grow into fully participating members of the world community.

The conference also saw the launch of a new prize – the Michael Jackson International Children's Prize. Guests were told:

> This programme will fund a new international prize designed to put the brightest 'spotlight' in the world on those individuals who are working on children's issues. With the awarding of this prize, the Foundation will make the people of the world and their political, economic and social communities aware of the most important needs of children.
>
> The prize will be awarded to those individuals and their organizations who have done the most on a grass-roots level to help children at risk and to heal the world. Each year, via a rigorous selection process, individuals will be nominated for the prize by the world's leading children's organizations and an anonymous group of individuals working in the field of children's issues. Then six recipients, one from each of the inhabited continents, will be selected by a jury to receive the prize. The prize will be a cash award of $65,000 to each individual and his/her organization. The prize-winners will receive their awards at a ceremony that will be covered by the international press.

The Heal the World organizers also launched a second programme, which they called the World Council of Children. This was to be a forum for children to express their vision, hopes and thoughts to the world from their unique perspective. Council meetings would also enable children to learn about issues that affect them and the world. Organizers said the Heal the World Foundation would be working with other leading children's organizations, such as UNICEF, Save the Children Federation and CARE.

Talking about the Heal the World tour, Jackson said:

'We hope to raise around £75 million from the tour. Getting money for the charity is really the main reason I am going on the road again. Children are the future of the world. We can learn so much of them. But we need to help them all we can.'

He also frequently visits children in hospitals to which he makes regular, large donations. When the *Dangerous* tour began, I was informed by sources close to the star that Jackson would be playing Florence Nightingale, visiting sick children in hospitals throughout the world while he was on the road. He would also be donating money to many of them so they could build special wards which he hoped would be named after him.

The tour will see him call into different children's hospitals in every city he plays in. Michael will not only be brightening up the lives of sick children everywhere by his appearances but will be presenting fat cheques worth hundreds of thousands of pounds to the hospitals. When he comes to London next month he is set to call in on one of the world's most famous children's hospitals at Great Ormond Street.

During his stay in Munich he will present the mayor of the city with a cheque for £30,000 to help children's hospitals there. Much of the money he donates during his hospital treks will be enough to build special Michael Jackson rooms, filled with his own personally chosen toys in the children's wards. In Rotterdam a Michael Jackson room has already been built which he will open when the tour goes there next week.

A spokesman for the singer added: 'It's a wonderful gesture . . . Michael simply adores children and wants to do everything he can to help them. When the tour ends in eighteen months' time, there will be plenty of Michael Jackson rooms in hospitals all over the world.'

Some rumours of Jackson's obsession with children *have* bordered on the bizarre. Jackson was said to have struck a deal with one hospital where he donated funds to their paediatric unit in exchange for witnessing the birth of new-born babies. He was said to have liked to look into the eyes of children emerging into the world so that he could look into their souls.

One of Jackson's first childhood friends was child-actor Emmanuel Lewis. The relationship became public when he began turning up to parties and functions with the boy, who was eleven years old when they first met. The singer had seen Lewis, a midget, in his hit comedy series, 'Webster', and rang up his mother to invite her son to visit him while he was making his breath-taking *Thriller* video in 1983. From then on the strange twosome became a regular sight, with Jackson often carrying Lewis, who was just three foot four inches in height, in his arms like a big baby. But both Jackson's aides and Lewis's family began to worry as the friendship developed — Jackson even took Lewis along with him on his dates with actress Brooke Shields — and Michael began lavishing gifts on his little friend. Lewis's former speech coach, Vivian Greene, admitted: 'They weren't happy because of the way it looked, especially when Michael began buying presents.'

The friendship was reportedly stopped by Lewis's mother, who said that what had started as a friendship had turned into 'an obsession' after she found out that the singer and Lewis had checked in the Los Angeles Four Seasons hotel as father and son.

Lewis made no comment about the recent allegations that have plagued Jackson or about the time they spent together. All he said was: 'The fun things we did are secrets shared by me and Michael.'

What had begun as a fascination with Lewis turned into an obsession with many other young boys – an obsession that was to plunge Jackson headlong into scandal. Another of Michael's young playmates was child-actor Jonathan Spence. Michael met Jonathan, then ten, on the set of the seventeen-minute Disney feature *Captain Eo*, a fantasy short directed by Francis Ford Coppola in 1985. The two hung out with each other during the shooting. Sources who were working on the set at the time revealed how Jackson loved being around Spence and how they would mess around in between the scenes, throwing food at each other. The young boy even accompanied Michael to the hospital one afternoon in July of that year when he sprained his wrist. They became very close and often people would see them arm-in-arm or even hugging and kissing. But their friendship came to an end with the close of filming.

Another of Jackson's friends was Corey Feldman, the heart-throb star of *Stand By Me*. Feldman, now twenty-two, admitted that he slept in the same bedroom as the singer when he was thirteen years old but insisted that nothing sexual ever went on between them. 'Michael and I were great friends. There was no sexual connotation. We talked every day. And we slept in the same room and hung out.' As the scandal fermented, Feldman hit out against the child abuse allegations levelled against Jackson: 'I was molested as a child and I know the difference. Maybe if we were watching TV, we fell asleep in the same bed. But it was just a warm friendship, that was all.'

In 1988 ten-year-old Jimmy Safechuck became the envy of millions of children all over the world. He was the boy that singer Michael Jackson befriended on his year-long world tour which followed in the wake of the *Bad* album. Safechuck was to become Jackson's most visible and long-lasting friend until the singer met Jordan Chandler. Everywhere that Jackson went, so did Safechuck –

even on stage. The superstar had the bondage-style outfit that he wore on stage made in Safechuck's size so the little boy could become a miniature double. Safechuck, who stayed in his own suite close to Jackson's wherever the Jackson entourage pitched camp during the tour, even basked in the limelight himself. Jackson pushed the boy on to the balcony of his London hotel as the adoring fans chanted the singer's name down below. One fan, who had been waiting outside the plush Mayfair hotel since the early hours of the morning for a glimpse of the superstar, said: 'Michael was having the time of his life. He thought it would be a real laugh to put Jimmy over there in front of all the screaming fans. Jimmy seemed to love it. He really coped easily with being in the limelight and waved to us all down below, just like a real star.'

Jackson, then twenty-nine, and Safechuck became friends after they worked together on one of the singer's Pepsi adverts. Soon after, Jackson asked Safechuck to come on tour with him. A source close to Jackson revealed at the time: 'Michael loves being in the company of children. He just feels more at home with them perhaps because in many ways he is a child himself. And he is really taken with little Jimmy. Jimmy is quite a showman himself and very funny. He makes Michael laugh. The two have become quite inseparable.'

Safechuck accompanied Jackson to some of the best toy shops when they were on the European leg of the tour. At the world-famous Hamleys in London's Regent Street the singer splashed out some thousands of pounds on toys – including several computer games – for himself and his pal. They also went on a whole parade of funfair rides together. At the time, though people might have seen that relationship as odd, no one alluded to any sexual aspects to it. The source added: 'Jimmy and Michael often walk around town, holding hands and laughing like a couple of schoolboys. But there is nothing sinister behind it. Michael is just like an older brother to him.' The bottom line, then, was simply that Michael was weird and that having young boys around him was just another of his eccentricities like playing with his animals or collecting mannequins. Indeed, for a long time their friendship seemed quite natural: many people assumed that Safechuck was one of Jackson's distant cousins, an assumption that was made with many of his boy friends.

It was later claimed that Michael Jackson has been paying money out regularly to Safechuck and his family. A source of mine in Los Angeles alleged: 'Whenever Michael was through with a kid he would pay them off. Jimmy Safechuck was paid off.'

Jackson was said to have paid for Safechuck's acting and directing lessons. And it was claimed that his father – now the wealthy owner of a rubbish disposal business in the San Fernando Valley – had been paid vast amounts of money. Another source said: 'Michael picks up all the expenses for Jimmy and his parents. They receive a good cheque from Jackson regularly. I'm not sure of the exact amount but it's very generous.'

Jack Gordon confirmed that Jackson paid the Safechucks 'hush' money. Another source said of Jimmy:

He was Michael's best friend for a long time and then Michael just lost interest in him. He became upset and jealous when Michael turned his attention away from him and on to someone else. Suddenly this wonderful world that he was living in, in which he was lavished with all kinds of presents and meeting all sorts of celebrities, was snatched away from him . . . Michael agreed he would pay for counselling for Jimmy and also paid for him to have lessons in acting and directing.

Child-star Macaulay Culkin was the most famous of Jackson's friends. Millionaire Culkin, whose starring roles in such films as *Home Alone* sent millions of girls under the age of twelve weak at the knees, was a platonic playmate of Jackson's for over a year. At the age of eleven, the blond-haired, angelic-looking boy met the singer when he appeared in Jackson's most spectacular video – the one which accompanied his 'Black or White' single. Culkin played a guitar-toting schoolboy.

It was later alleged that Jackson used the videos and films he made as an excuse for auditioning hundreds of young good-looking boys. Jackson was reported to be so fond of Culkin that, in addition to the usual shopping expeditions to toy stores, he bought him a brand-new Corvette sports car worth £35,000 and then paid an extra £6,500 to have it converted into a bed. There were even rumours that Jackson had offered to build a home for Culkin's family next door to his ranch.

It was at the ranch that a home video was shot of the two of them larking around and having water pistol fights. In one part of the film Jackson shouts like an excited schoolboy: 'I want the world to know I won the water fight with my friend Mac.' And Culkin yells back: 'No you didn't, you're drenched.' And, just like kids who sulk when they lose, Jackson feigns annoyance and tells Culkin: 'You're such a knucklehead! . . . I'm walking my pet monkey Bubbles.'

Culkin talked about the fun and the mischief that he and Jackson got up to whenever they were together. They would spend hours on the phone to each other almost every night. He said: 'When I spend time at his place, we play tricks on each other and on his security guards. Michael calls every night usually, maybe every other night. He's cool. He's a lot like me. We go to video arcades, we like animals, carnivals, and four-wheeled motor cycles. We like goofing off.'

Though it has been adamantly denied that there was anything sexual between Jackson and Culkin, their intense friendship apparently worried Culkin's parents once the stories of child abuse surfaced. Rumour has it that Jackson was ordered not to see Culkin again. Culkin's father Kit refused to be drawn on the matter, however, merely saying: 'Michael and my son are friends – just friends. Any suggestion that Michael was anything but a friend is completely untrue.' Though since the scandal their friendship seems to have been put completely on ice.

At one time Jackson's fascination with children was seen as totally innocent, but it is unlikely that it can ever be viewed in that light again. An incident described in J. Randy Tarborelli's book is prophetic. It took place when Jackson was nineteen, making his movie *The Wiz*, and sharing an apartment in New York with LaToya. A friend called Theresa recalled how: 'We all sat around and talked about child abuse. Michael was fascinated by the subject. He wanted to know everything we girls had ever heard or read about it. He said he liked to read about child abuse as much as he could.'

But many believe there is nothing sinister behind his fondness for children. British singer Thomas Dolby had a first-hand experience of Jackson's strange fascination for children when he was invited into Jackson's home. He recently told me:

It was around the time when 'Billie Jean' and my record 'She Blinded Me With Science' were both high in the American top five and we were both working with the same video company. Michael invited me over to his house and, when I got there, there was a very strange scene going on. Michael was sitting in this huge medieval throne wearing a kind of silk lounge suit and there were about a dozen little kids running around in their pyjamas. They were playing all kinds of games and Michael seemed to be orchestrating the whole episode. It was very strange . . . I talked to him quite a lot then and I found him a touchingly human character. I have to say that I don't actually think he is guilty of the sex abuse charges. I can't imagine Michael Jackson getting aroused, to be honest. I think he is probably asexual. I know it is hard for people to imagine that there are people who aren't entirely motivated by sex because so many people are. But I also think that too much is made of him being childlike and having childish qualities. I think he is definitely a grown-up. I think he is very articulate and knows what he is doing.

Dolby has another connection with Jackson – his manager, Mary Coller, was Jackson's personal assistant for three years. Coller, like a number of loyal Jackson employees, was sacked with barely a handshake after devoted service. Dolby comments:

I think his constant boy companions really started to happen after Mary left. It certainly wasn't happening to that extent while she was there. Mary's view is that he is a lonely guy and children were one kind of companion he found easy to get on with. Jackson was always very suspicious of adults, not surprisingly, as there were an awful lot who seemed to take advantage of him. He found it a lot easier to relate to kids. Mary has had visits from the police about the child abuse allegations but all she could tell them was that after three years of working with him, she never saw anything that she would consider improper.

But there is no doubt that Jackson wins the hearts of children not just because of the games he plays with them or the love he heaps on them, but also because they are showered with toys and gifts. Children, just like anyone else, can be bought and it is naive to think otherwise. And Jackson is a walking toy emporium. His shopping expeditions take him to children's shops all over the world, which open up especially for him, so he can buy whatever goodies take his fancy. Some toys are larger than others: he bought funfair carousel rides on his visits to Europe and transported them back to his personal Disneyland, where they sat with his other rides. No toy is ever too grand or too expensive to buy for a child he is fond of.

Much of Jackson's love for children can be seen in a selfish light: there is no getting away from the fact that the singer gets a thrill from being around children. But many of his relationships with children *are* purely altruistic. The singer recently considered starting up a children's TV channel, and has raised millions of pounds for children all over the world – he recently helped the children of war-torn Bosnia when he sent £93,000 worth of relief supplies to the country. Many such acts of philanthropy are never reported in the media.

This is why the scandal surrounding Jackson is such a thorny dilemma. Whatever alleged harm Jackson has done to a small handful of children, the good that he has done to millions more should not be completely negated by the smears against him.

CHAPTER 9

Affairs of the Heart

MICHAEL JACKSON'S SEX LIFE has always been something of a mystery, and that is the way he has liked to keep it. Many people, like the singer Thomas Dolby, saw him as asexual; others saw him as androgynous – neither wholly male or female but somewhere in between; while others saw him as a sexual innocent whose experiences of sexuality were those of a small child. Very few people thought of Michael Jackson as a sexual creature. When he grabbed his crotch, thrust his pelvis out, or gyrated his hips, he was just play-acting, that was all. He once said of being a sex symbol: 'I think it's fun that girls think I'm sexy but it's all just fantasy. I like to make my fans happy so I pose and dance in a way that makes them think I'm romantic, but really I'm not that way.' Madonna may have been sexually threatening, but to most people Jackson had all the sexual power of a eunuch. These asexual myths had grown up around the star not just through rumours, gossip or the confidences of friends but through Jackson himself, who promulgated tales of his own sexual naivety. In fact the androgynous aura Jackson manufactured for himself was thought by many to be an image loved by children and parents alike because it was not sexually threatening. It might have been sexy on the outside, but it seemed perfectly safe on the inside.

He once made a startling confession to me during an intimate interview. He revealed that he was still a virgin: 'I have never had an adult relationship. I have never made love. I don't want to just yet. There so many other things I want to do.'

At the time I was shocked that such a pop idol, who had girls pursuing him wherever he went, had not made love to one yet. I put it down to four things: firstly, I believed that Michael Jackson had never had a real childhood and that this made him childlike, with an innocence that infused his whole life, including his sensual life; secondly, at the time I met him he claimed to be a devout Jehovah's Witness – along with his mother, Katherine, he was said to be the most religious of the Jacksons – and as such did not believe in sex before marriage: 'The bible doesn't approve of things like that. There are some very direct words about sex in the bible, and I believe them.' Thirdly, Jackson was an amazing workaholic. Workaholics are known for repressing their sex life in favour of their career. Jackson himself told me: 'I just don't have the time to have a steady girlfriend. My career comes first.'

And fourthly, I believed that he could have been reacting against all the things he saw when he was a child. And he certainly saw some seedy show-business sights. He told me:

Ever since I was young, I've been surrounded by strange sights. Like fans ripping off their coats, and standing nude in front of me. And being sent mountains of sexy letters with every kind of suggestion in them. You wouldn't believe some of the things that I saw at an early age. One of the worst memories that I'll never erase is a stripper who played the same club we did when I was six. She was called Rose Marie. After she had taken everything off she pushed her underwear in the faces of the audience and made them sniff it. It was disgusting. By the time I reached my teens I guess I'd been exposed to most grown-up things.

At an early age Jackson himself was thrust into sex play in the dives where the Jackson Five played as they tried to hustle their way up the first rungs of the show-business ladder. His father had devised a stage routine which included a sexually crude act: at the end of a song the young Michael had to go into the audience, crawl under the tables and lift up the women's skirts.

There were other people who believed that, in addition to the sexual forwardness that Jackson saw all around him, he was bothered by the sexual promiscuity of those closest to him – like his father and his brothers. His father had a number of affairs, while his brothers took full advantage of the groupies that chased them on tour. They even made love to them in the room they shared with Jackson as the young boy vainly tried to sleep. At times Jackson became so upset at their constant philandering that he begged the girls who came backstage not to allow his brothers to take advantage of them.

Jackson also admitted that his relationships with women had been hampered because of his suspicions of adults: 'It's hard just making friends, but as far as romance is concerned, it's even harder. With so many girls around, how am I ever going to know? Being an entertainer, you can't tell who is your friend. That's why most of the time, I'd rather be by myself than with anyone else.'

Years after he did his interview with me he was still confessing to being a virgin on TV in his famous interview with Oprah Winfrey, although this time he was more bashful. When Winfrey asked him if he was a virgin, the thirty-four-year-old star looked flustered before he remonstrated: 'How can you ask me that question? I'm a gentleman. It is something that is private. It shouldn't be spoken about.

You can call me old-fashioned, but I can't talk about that.' It was his way of not so much avoiding the issue as subtly letting the public know that he was still a sexual innocent.

For a time the only hints that his hormones had not been completely sedated came through his relationships with two kinds of women. The first were women who were old enough to be his mother – Diana Ross, Jane Fonda and Elizabeth Taylor. Jackson says that he feels safer being around older women: 'I only feel safe and relaxed when I am in the company of an older woman who has the understanding of a mother. The beauty of a woman needs time to mature and blossom. A young woman tastes much like unripened fruit but an older woman has more sweetness, character and understanding. I prefer to have relationships with women who understand me and respect me for the person I am and not because of my pop success.'

But he also went out with young girls, child-stars like himself, such as Tatum O'Neal and Brooke Shields. To the more cynical it seems telling that the only women Jackson has been 'romantically' attached to have been big showbiz stars. They find it most odd that the singer has never yet been seen on a date with a woman who has not been a celebrity of some kind.

The first woman in his life after his mother was the beautiful singer Diana Ross, whom Jackson stayed with when he and his brothers first came to Los Angeles. He loved talking to Diana about all the new experiences he was having and she – being a practised show-business trouper – would offer him advice on how to cope with his new-found stardom. He once confessed about his school-boy crush on Diana: 'I was in love with Diana. She's older than me, but so what? At one time, I thought I wanted to marry her. You fall in love with a person, a chemistry, a mind, a soul – not a birth certificate, not a date of birth . . . I owe a lot to her. She's helped me a great deal. We were very close.'

Next up was Jane Fonda, who was seen as another surrogate mother. He met the actress, who is now involved with CNN boss Ted Turner, in the late seventies around the time he sacked his father as manager. She provided him with the comfort that he needed at a time when family life seemed to be disintegrating. There were even rumours of a romance between the two, but they were far-fetched and ill-informed. Jackson visited her while she was filming *On Golden Pond*. According to Fonda, who at one time was helping Jackson with his acting lessons:

> We talked and talked and talked. His intelligence is instinctual and emotional, like a child's. If any artist loses that childlikeness, you lose a lot of creative juice. So Michael creates around himself a world that protects his creativity . . . Michael is an extremely fragile person. I think just getting on with life and making contact with other people is hard for him. He's happiest when he's in a role. He's like Peter Pan.

Jackson's most important mother-figure is Hollywood legend Elizabeth Taylor. The couple had a lot in common. Both were huge child-stars, both were sensitive, and both, it was said, were victims of child abuse. Taylor, who married her current, eighth husband Larry Fortenski at the singer's Neverland ranch, always speaks of Michael in pure hyperbole. She once wrote in *Dancing the Dream*, a book of poems by Jackson: 'When I hear the name Michael Jackson, I think of brilliance, of dazzling stars, lasers and deep emotions, I adore Michael Jackson.'

Those who have worked closely with Jackson, like Jennifer Batten, a guitarist in his backing band on his last tour, spoke of how Jackson and Taylor always looked so at ease together; with other women he always seemed nervous:

I saw Liza Minelli, Sophia Loren and Brooke Shields all hanging around his dressing-room, but he was so embarrassed and shy when they were around him that he hardly said a word to anyone. But with Elizabeth, it was completely different. The two got on famously. Whenever I saw them together on the last tour, they always had huge smiles on their faces.

Taylor's love and undying loyalty and friendship were demonstrated when she helped Jackson throughout the ordeal of the sex abuse allegations. She was the first of his friends to give him the support he so badly needed. She flew out, together with her husband Larry Fortenski, to see the singer even before his family did. In spite of her own ill health, Taylor made the twenty-one-hour journey from Los Angeles to Singapore on Jackson's birthday and arrived for the concert worn out but determined not to miss the show. She told aides: 'I can't let Michael down. I am dog-tired but I have to be there.' She was driven to the stadium in a limousine and then transferred to a golf cart to be taken inside the stadium. After the show a touched Jackson told her: 'You're the best present I could have had.' The source added: 'Elizabeth is a true friend to Michael, as soon as the scandal broke she was on the phone to him, telling him he could depend on her and she would be there on his birthday.'

Taylor, knowing how emotionally fragile and delicate Jackson could be, proved she was no fair-weather friend. She said that she believed the singer was innocent of the child abuse allegations and was the victim of a destructive blackmail attempt:

I believe totally that Michael will be vindicated. I believe in Michael's integrity, his love and his respect of children. He's here all alone and he's going though a terrible time. I just wanted to be with him. I believe what is happening to Michael is extortion. And if it is, those responsible must be made to pay. This is a horrible thing for Michael to go through. But I believe one hundred per cent in his integrity – he'd rather cut his own wrist than harm a child.

At the end of 1993, when Jackson did his disappearing trick, it was Taylor who helped him out once again. Reports stated that he had phoned her from Mexico, begging her to 'Get me out of here, now, please.' She responded immediately. Jackson, apparently battling against his addiction, later gave thanks to a star who had had her own battles with drugs and alcohol: 'Elizabeth Taylor, my close friend, has been a source of strength and counsel as this crisis came about. I shall never forget her unconditional love in helping me through this period.'

Two of the most famous and the best orchestrated of Jackson's other relationships have been with Tatum O'Neal and Brooke Shields. He became friendly with Tatum when he was nineteen and the actress, who had just been awarded a Grammy for her role in *Paper Moon*, was thirteen. The two enjoyed each other's company for a little while and Jackson rather overdramatized things when he wrote in his autobiography, *Moonwalk*: 'I fell in love with her, and she with me, and we were very close for a long time. She was my first love after Diana.' Tatum insisted that her relationship with Jackson was strictly platonic, and he once told me: 'Tatum is just about my best buddy. We're not going steady, but we're friends. She and her dad have been great to me.'

Another platonic romance involved Brooke Shields, best known for her role in *The Blue Lagoon*, who has always publicly pledged to stay a virgin until the day she marries. Jackson once said of Brooke: 'She's my kind of girl. She's also a wonderful friend. One of the things that I love about her is that I can trust her and that's really important to me. One day I could even see myself marrying her.' His recent interview with Oprah Winfrey revealed: 'I date, I go out with girls. Right now I'm dating Brooke Shields. It's mostly at home. She comes over to my house and I go over to hers. I don't like to go out much. I have been in love. I'm in love with Brooke. I've always liked Brooke.'

This was in direct contradiction to the comment he made about taking Brooke Shields to the Grammys: 'She's okay. But I only took her to help her out. There was no romance. Not at all. We're friends.' Shields herself revealed just days after Jackson's Oprah Winfrey interview that there were crossed lines between her and Michael and their relationship was not what Michael had made it out to be:

> We have known each other since we were very young and we are very close. People have a tendency to misunderstand our relationship. It is definitely platonic and always has been. Michael called to ask whether he could name me if Oprah asked him who he loved. I told him it would be an honour. We love each other – but not like a boy and girlfriend.

And a little while later reports surfaced that Jackson had even paid Shields handsomely for their 'dates' together.

Michael's sister LaToya added her penny's worth to the romantic link with Brooke Shields. Talking on TV, she put an end to any rumour of wedding bells, even claiming: 'Brooke was the most aggressive female in his whole life. She used to come round to our house on occasions to spend time with Michael. He wasn't too happy because at the time he was very religious.'

Many of the stories about Jackson's 'romances' with women have either been publicity stunts or just gossip that papers have run knowing that the star who courts publicity would not be offended. One such item was his 'affair' with a casino dancer, Shoshana Hawley, on a trip he made to Las Vegas as part of his *Dangerous* tour in 1992. Jackson was said to have spent two days wooing the sexy twenty-five-year-old dancer after she was asked to give him a guided tour of the town. When the sightseeing was over, Jackson invited her back to his palatial suite at the plush Mirage Hotel where the pair shared steamed vegetables, rice and herbal tea. During his stay he also insisted she join him for four performances of top Vegas show, *King Arthur's Tournament* – in which she had formerly played a lead role. Shoshana even persuaded Jackson to watch a raunchy act featuring topless dancers at Bally's Hotel. A source commented: 'They were inseparable for forty-eight hours . . . They spent the whole time laughing, giggling and holding hands. They were like two lovestruck kids. Wherever Michael went Shoshana went too – even to his hotel. But it was obvious Shoshana was slightly more to Michael than a tour guide.'

But their romance was never mentioned again. There were also reports that he was dating his make-up artist, Karen Faye. He apparently admitted: 'We love each other deeply. I have never felt this way before.' But Karen scuppered any further rumours when she insisted that there was no romantic relationship between them. Other 'romances' included dancer Tatiana Thumtzen and backing singer Sheryl Crow. It was as if Jackson was encouraging the media to write anything they wanted about his romances with the opposite sex, and perhaps his camp even helped fuel some of them to give the star a more heterosexual image.

Author Randy Tarborelli says that in the course of his research for his exhaustive biography of Jackson he could not find any genuine romance that Jackson had had with a woman: 'Michael is a sexually confused innocent. By that I mean not one person from the hundreds of interviews I've done has said they have had an intimate relationship with him. It says a lot about Michael and his dreadful loneliness.'

The lack of any publicly visible romance in his life and his strange, effeminate appearance – helped by plastic surgery which has given him a softer, more feminine face with a smaller nose and higher cheekbones, and make-up consisting of bright red lipstick, plucked eyebrows and heavy black eyeliner – has led to much speculation that he is gay. Jackson has always angrily denied it: 'Those people who think I'm gay are wrong. I'm not. It's just a lot of gossip. People make up those rumours because they have nothing better to do.'

His one-time vocal coach, Seth Riggs, once recounted an incident that the singer had told him about: 'The other day a big, tall, nice-looking fellow came up to me and said, "Gee, Michael, I think you're wonderful. I sure would like to go to bed with you." I looked at him and said: "When was the last time you read the bible? You know, you really should read it because there is some real information in there about homosexuality."'

Jackson himself has stated: 'Some people think I'm gay because my voice is so high. But that is just a lot of gossip and that kind of gossip is not important.' And his mother Katherine has emphasized on many occasions: 'Michael isn't gay. It's against his religion. It's against God. The bible speaks against it.' His brother Jermaine says:

> There have been rumours that Michael is gay but that is complete rubbish. He has told me that someday he will settle down with a girl and have lots of babies. He goes out on dates but is very secretive about it because he does not want them to be messed up. In spite of all his success he needs lots of affection.

Michael's father Joe was once said to have questioned his son sternly about the gay allegations which had been plaguing him. He was reported to have told one of Michael's male friends to leave the family home during the argument and demanded angrily: 'Is it true what everyone says about you – that you're gay? You spend a lot of time with other young men.' But his son hit back: 'Don't you have any trust in me? I'm not gay.'

American reporter Denise Worrell once came across Jackson sitting close to a male friend in a darkened room. She had been interviewing Jackson's father for *Time* magazine. On a tour round the family home, Joe Jackson decided to let her see Michael's room as a treat. When he knocked on the bedroom door there was no answer. But Joe persisted, told Michael that he had someone with him he had wanted to meet, and asked if he could open the door. When he did so Worrell found herself in a completely dark room – the only light came from the glow of a TV set which Michael and his friend, a man in his twenties, were watching. Worrell said the singer appeared startled as he said hello. Afterwards, as she was leaving, she was brought back into the home and was told that Jackson's mother was prepared to do a short interview with her. During that interview Katherine Jackson poured cold water on the rumours that her son was gay and asked the reporter to help them: 'We were hoping you'd set the record straight and put a stop to the rumours. They say Michael is gay. He isn't. It's against his religion.'

There have been many rumours, too, that Jackson was sexually molested as a young boy, though the singer has always denied them. One such rumour claimed that Jackson's molestation happened at the hands of a Motown employee when the band were signed to the Motown label. Johnny Jackson, the Jacksons' cousin, admitted: 'They had lots of gay valets. When Michael was eleven one of them got sacked for touching up some of the boys' friends. Mother was upset, but I don't know if Michael had been touched up too.'

Much of Jackson's strangeness has been attributed to the star's relationship with his father. There is no doubt that Joe Jackson looms large in his son's life even to this day, though the two hardly see each other. It was Joe Jackson who made the Jackson Five a success. He drove his sons mercilessly, instilling in them his belief that only hard work and discipline could take them out of the Indiana ghetto where they lived. Jackson senior made them practise their music for hours every day, preventing them from leading a normal life. And if they stepped out of line they would be beaten.

In his autobiography, *Moonwalk*, Jackson said of his father:

> I still don't know him and that's sad for a son who hungers to know his father . . . Sometimes we could hear all the fun and excitement outside but we could never join in. My father's strictness and all the rehearsing we had for hours each day kept us out of trouble. Sometimes it was hard. We would be at a late night party where we had fallen asleep and he would shake us and make us start performing.

The rumours that Michael Jackson was a victim of child abuse have kept resurfacing. His sister LaToya has frequently punctured the image of the loving happy family which most other members of the clan try to promote. It was LaToya – the most rebellious of the Jackson children – who incurred the wrath of her family when she declared that Joe Jackson had sexually and physically abused his children. She said she was one of the children he had abused and was still suffering from the effects. A completely new and horrific picture was painted of the family's stern, harsh father. In her book, *LaToya Grows Up in the Jackson Family*, she branded him a 'monster' and she described the 'horrible beatings' she was given by her

father's 'terrible hand'. In this book, LaToya says her father
was guilty of child abuse, physical violence and psychological cruelty. She recalls an incident which took place when
she was six: Joe Jackson fell into a rage after reading a
school report card which said that, though her work was
excellent, she rarely spoke and the school had decided it
was best to keep her back a grade. Her father fell into such
a temper that he smacked her face with his open palm and
then beat her with his metal-buckled belt. She screamed
for him to stop. She wrote:

> If I close my eyes, I can still see his face. His eyes
> turned cat's-eye yellow. His forehead seemed to
> stretch back to the middle of his head. It was as if
> he'd been transformed into a monster. 'You will
> never shame me like this again. Never,' he yelled,
> punctuating his words with hard slaps. 'This will
> teach you to study.' Joseph – who'd once been a
> professional boxer – pummelled my face with his
> fists. I cried till my eyes were nearly swollen shut.

LaToya also described how her father's fury erupted and
boiled over against the other children: 'He often whipped
my brothers until they collapsed. Michael was never
allowed to grow up in a normal way – none of us was.
Apart from being in the spotlight from an early age, he
was deeply affected by my father's brutality. It wasn't just
the physical abuse that got to Michael, it was the mental
strain that our father put on him.'

She described a family who, far from praying together
and staying together, were at war with each other – a
family who rowed incessantly and who hated Joe Jackson.

Michael, much of whose childhood was spent away
from the mother he adored as he and his brothers travelled
across America to seek fame and fortune, has also claimed
that his father beat him and that at times made him so

terrified that he would be physically sick. He later learned how to stop his father's beatings when they got too severe: he would threaten never to sing again – and Joe Jackson recognized the seriousness of the threat all too plainly. Johnny Jackson, a cousin who lived with the family, recalled: 'He would hit us if we didn't do what he said. But Michael stood up to him. After a while if Joe threatened to beat him Michael said he'd never sing again and Joe left off.'

In 1988, as tensions between the father and Michael increased, Jackson senior admitted: 'I may have to go and get him and let him know he has a family still. I can always drag him out of there. He ain't ever going to get too big for me to go get him. And he knows I'll come and get him too.'

Joe Jackson's brazen infidelities also left Michael scarred. Frequently his father would say goodnight to his sons and then rush back to his bedroom with a strange woman. Jackson's brother Marlon admitted: 'Joe thought it was funny, but we were very upset by it.' And Jackson was even more horrified when he learnt that his father had an illegitimate child by Cheryl Terrell, with whom he had an affair in 1973 when she was twenty-five and he was forty-five. Michael Jackson's half-sister was born on 30 August 1974, the day after his sixteenth birthday.

His father's infidelities caused Jackson's mother Katherine to file for divorce but the divorce never took place and for many years Katherine put up with her erring husband and the sham that their marriage had become.

But some close friends of the family deny that Joe Jackson was a violent man and say he was just a strict disciplinarian. The long-suffering Katherine says: 'He wasn't an ogre. He was just a hard-nosed disciplinarian who wanted our children to get the most from their God-given talents.'

Despite his early experiences and the example set by his parents' marriage, despite all the asexual and sexual innuendo about him, Michael Jackson has always maintained that one day he will marry: I would love to get married one day. I don't believe in sex before marriage. I'm very conservative in my outlook and I'm not ashamed of it. When I do marry it will be to a good old-fashioned girl. Someone like my mother. I compare all women with my mother. It's hard for any woman to follow her. My mom is a league all of her own.' He was still at it during the Oprah Winfrey interview when he told the TV presenter: 'I want to marry and have children. I would feel as if my life is incomplete if I do not. It's my dream, but at the moment I'm married to my life and my music.'

Whatever the reasons Jackson gave to explain his sexual innocence – whether it was his religion, his lack of trust in people, or whether it was that he simply could not meet the right girl – the more cynical could say that it was a calculated front. Those believing the allegations against the singer would say that his declarations were a perfect smokescreen behind which he could hide in the pursuit of his obsession and fascination with young boys. And so the more Jackson repeated, in those apparently brutal and honest self-revelations, that he was a sexual virgin – not something that most people would want to boast about – the more likely it was that the public would be hoodwinked and so leave him free to indulge in his alleged affairs with young boys.

True to his childlike persona,
Jackson is a devotee of all the Disney characters.

British supermodel Naomi Campbell starred with
Jackson in his *In the Closet* video.

Top right: The self-proclaimed King of Pop exits Wembley Stadium in characteristically flamboyant fashion.

Left and above left: Two electrifying moments from the *Dangerous* tour show why Jackson is acknowledged as one of the world's most exciting stage performers.

On stage, Jackson once confessed, is the one place where he feels most at home.

At the Soul Train Awards in 1993
Jackson picked up three prizes –
but had to appear in a wheelchair
thanks to a sprained ankle.

The 1993 Grammy Awards saw
Jackson pick up yet another tribute
to his extraordinary musical genius.

An emotional moment at Bill Clinton's inauguration ceremony in Washington, in January 1992.

Jordan Chandler, his mother June and his half-sister Lily accompany Jackson to the World Music Awards in Monte Carlo in May 1993.

The four of them enjoy the show with Prince Albert of Monaco. Jackson later picked up three awards himself.

Bodyguards leap to Jackson's aid as a fan lunges towards the star at the end of the evening and he falls to the ground.

Gloria Allred, one of the lawyers engaged by Jordan Chandler and his father to bring a suit for damages against Jackson.

A revealing portrait of Jackson, snapped during a charity event in New York in 1993.

Sam Emerson, one of Jackson's official photographers,
took this portrait of the enigmatic star.

CHAPTER 10

The Settlement

MICHAEL JACKSON'S AMBITIOUS *DANGEROUS* TOUR, launched with such huge publicity, turned out to be a disaster. The performances which he did manage to give were not all successes and his attempts at publicity stunts often misfired. After the scandal came out, nothing seemed to go right for him. There were more woes to come. Not long after he cancelled the tour, Pepsi announced that its $10-million sponsorship deal with the singer was over. And songwriters Bob Smith and Reynard Jones alleged that Jackson had stolen three of his biggest hits, 'Thriller', 'We Are the World' and 'The Girl Is Mine', from them.

Then, as 1993 drew to a close, Jackson was hit by a series of potentially crippling financial blows. A children's charity, the Children's Peace Foundation, began an action again the star for £100 million. The charity claimed that Jackson had cheated on multi-million-dollar marketing deals and skimmed cash from them. The Foundation issued its claims for damages at the same Los Angeles court where the child abuse allegations had been filed. Michael Jackson's life was fast becoming the embodiment of the old adage, 'It never rains but it pours.' The charity's chief, Peter Georgi, said at the time: 'This is a bigger problem for Michael than the child abuse case. We are not talking about the word of a boy. These are documented frauds and theft on a grand scale.'

The charity was formed in 1984 by Los Angeles businessman Georgi; its honorary advisers included Mohammed Ali, who was the Foundation's chairman, Jack Nicholson, Michael Douglas, Rod Stewart and Michael Cain, and its first donation was made by Hollywood director Steven Spielberg. In a 500-page dossier, the charity outlined the charges in minute detail: Jackson was alleged to have illegally resold the rights on products such as clothes, watches, sunglasses and sweets, which he had endorsed and which the charity believed it owned. The star and his business advisers were accused of twenty cases of wrong-doing, including fraud, racketeering, stealing trade secrets, and breach of contract. The lawsuit stated: 'This complaint seeks to remedy the enormous damages done by a pervasive pattern of fraud for which Michael Jackson appears to be primarily responsible.'

A few days later another lawsuit was served on the luckless star. This time top promoter Marcel Avram sued him for £13 million over the cancellation of his world tour, which had resulted in Jackson scrapping nineteen concerts. He accused the singer of fraud and breach of contract, claiming that Jackson had withheld details of his addiction to morphine and pethidine when he signed for the tour. Furthermore Avram claimed that Jackson had failed to reveal the sex abuse allegations that were brewing up against him, quickly plunging the whole tour into chaos.

The child abuse allegations had, according to Avram, impaired Jackson's singing when he did appear on stage; he was so preoccupied that the shows were below contracted standards. He also said that Jackson had hardly rehearsed for the second leg of the tour, and only decided to begin it the day police searched his ranch. The Munich-based concert promoter, who had launched Jackson's *Bad* tour of 1988, revealed that the superstar was paid a £1.3-million advance for the tour and was to receive £3 million for the concerts and 85 per cent of the profits. He alleged that Jackson's backers had refused to pay outstanding bills and reimburse the millions of dollars advanced for the cancelled shows; he himself had been sued by promoters who lost money because of the cancellation. Avram's lawyer, Don Engel, said: 'Michael Jackson has yet to pay one nickel to the people stranded after cancelling his world tour. He hung my client out to dry. We had no alternative but to bring the suit against him.' Avram added: 'He collected over $2 million in advances, $900,000 of which is for dates that he didn't perform.'

These lawsuits, and the others that had been issued against him – including one by the five sacked security guards and another by the two songwriters – meant that Jackson, a multi-millionaire, could be facing financial ruin; he could become a pauper. It was calculated that the outstanding legal actions against him totalled £150 million and the figure could double if other threatened actions went ahead. Legal expert Paul Ritchley said: 'His wealth could evaporate overnight.' Among those threatened lawsuits could be ones from seven other boys who, it was said, had been questioned by police about their relationships with Michael Jackson. A show-business lawyer also commented: 'If the plaintiffs in any of these suits get a fraction of what they are demanding, he would go bankrupt.'

Just a few days before Christmas 1993, on 22 December, Jackson gave the performance of his life. This performance involved no singing, no moonwalking and no crotch-grabbing. For the singer had finally decided to speak out at length for the first time about the scandal that had besieged him for the last few months. His speech was given, not in a courtroom or to police officers, but to the TV cameras. Jackson, the master performer, knew that television could be dramatically used to his advantage, so he invited the cameras of CNN into his Neverland home. He had been told by aides that he must appear more open and talkative: the days of hide-and-seek and silence had to be put aside, at least for the time being.

The speech was laden with emotion; Jackson begged the world to stop treating him like a criminal because he was innocent. He avoided discussing the allegations and managed to cast himself as a victim. Millions of people, glued to TV sets all over the world, heard his speech:

My deepest gratitude for your love and support. I am doing well and I am strong. As you may already know, after my tour ended I remained out of the country undergoing treatment for dependency on pain medication. This medication was initially prescribed to ease the excruciating pain that I was suffering after my recent reconstructive surgery on my scalp. There have been many disgusting statements made recently concerning allegations of improper conduct on my part. These statements about me are totally false. As I have maintained from the very beginning, I am hoping for a speedy end to this horrifying experience to which I have been subjected. I shall not in this statement respond to all of the false allegations being made against me. My lawyers have advised me that this is not the proper forum in which to do that.

I will say that I am particularly upset at the handling of this matter by the incredible, terrible mass media. At every opportunity the media has dissected and manipulated these allegations to reach their own conclusions. I ask all of you to wait to hear the truth before you label or condemn me. Don't treat me like a criminal, because I am innocent.

I have been forced to submit to a dehumanizing and humiliating examination by the Santa Barbara

County Sheriff's Department and the Los Angeles Police Department earlier this week. They served a search warrant on me which allowed them to view and photograph my body, including my penis, my buttocks, my lower torso, thighs and any other area that they wanted. They were supposedly looking for any discoloration, spotting, blotches or other evidence of a skin-colour disorder called vitiligo, which I have previously spoken about. The warrant also directed me to co-operate in any examination of my body by their decision, to determine the condition of my skin, to determine whether I have vitiligo or any other skin disorder. The warrant further stated that I had no right to refuse the examination or photographs, and if I failed to co-operate with them they would introduce that refusal at any trial as an indication of my guilt.

It was the most humiliating ordeal of my life, one that no person should have to suffer, and even after experiencing the indignity of the search the parties involved were still not satisfied and wanted to take even more pictures. It was a nightmare, it was a horrifying nightmare, but if this is what I have to endure to prove my innocence, my complete innocence, so be it. Throughout my life I have only tried to help thousands and thousands of children to live happy lives. It brings tears to my eyes to see any child who suffers. I am not guilty of these allegations, but if I am guilty of anything it is of giving all that I have to give to help children all over the world. It is of loving children of all ages and races, of gaining sheer joy from seeing children with their innocent and smiling faces. It is of enjoying through them the childhood that I missed myself. If I am guilty of anything it is of believing what God said about children: 'Suffer little children to come unto me and forbid them not, for such is the Kingdom of Heaven.' In no way do I think that I am God, but I do try to be God-like in my heart.

I am totally innocent of any wrong-doing and I know these terrible allegations will all be proven false. Again, to my friends and fans, thank you very much for all of your support. Together we will see this thing to the very end. I love you very much and may God bless you all. I love you. Goodbye.

It was a tear-jerking speech and it gave great hope to all Jackson's millions of fans around the world that he would not be dragged down by the allegations.

A few days after Christmas, singer Barbra Streisand made her first non-charity appearance for over twenty years and Michael Jackson was there. Streisand had quit the concert circuit because she was petrified about performing live; she also felt that live shows fell short of her high standards. But now she had come back in a fanfare of glory and publicity. The two Las Vegas concerts – attended by a host of celebrities, were set to earn her a staggering £13.6 million. Tickets for the show cost up to £680, but ticket touts had been selling them for up to £3,500.

Jackson was spotted in Las Vegas by holiday-makers as he was given a guided tour of the recently opened Treasure Island Resort Hotel by hotelier Stephen Wynn. There he met up with another old friend, the former junk-bond king, Michael Milken. The last time the pair had met was in March: Milken, after nearly two years in prison for fraud, was launching a children's TV channel with Jackson, who said: 'Milken is my friend because he has been through the fire, as I have, and emerged better for the process. He's been my friend because he has been misunderstood, as I have been, and hastily judged by those who had no right to assume that they knew this man without spending an hour in his company.' Little was Jackson to know that, a few months on, he himself was to be burnt by even worse fires.

Jackson's first live public appearance since he went into hiding came at a civil rights award ceremony organized by the National Association for the Advancement of Colored People on 5 January 1994. During this surprise appearance, Jackson gave a short but emotional speech, which could have been taken word for word from some legal drama, again protesting his innocence:

> Not only am I presumed to be innocent, I am innocent. Everyone is presumed to be innocent, until they are charged with a crime and then convicted by a jury of their peers. I never really took the time to understand the importance of that ideal until now, until I became the victim of false allegations and the willingness of others to exploit the worst until they have had a chance to hear the truth. But I am not fighting this battle alone. Together we will see it through.

Jackson's speech was greeted by a wildly cheering crowd. He was on stage, wearing a blue and gold outfit, to present an award for choreography at the Pasadena ceremony in which singer Whitney Houston scooped a handful of prizes, including 'Entertainer of the Year'.

But despite his protestations of innocence and his claims that he had nothing to hide, Michael Jackson refused to answer one single important question in a detailed questionnaire that Jordan Chandler's legal team presented to him. This contained 200 questions relating to Jackson's relationships with Jordan and other young boys. Jackson was asked why he spent 100 consecutive nights in bed alone with Jordan and why former employees were backing up the claims that he had molested children. Other

questions included whether it was normal for a thirty-
five-year-old man to sleep with young boys on such a
regular basis, and whether the singer had ever paid hush
money to silence the parents of young boys he entertained
at his home. But the only answers Jackson gave to the
questionnaire were his name and his date of birth. Feldman commented: 'Mr Jackson has used his worldwide
fame and his media access to loudly proclaim his innocence
and his supposed desire for a speedy resolution. However,
his conduct bespeaks quite a different intent – to delay and
frustrate the judicial process. He is clearly stone-walling.
There are certain vital questions he must answer.'

Jackson refused to answer the questions on the grounds
that he could incriminate himself: as an American citizen,
Jackson can plead the fifth amendment. According to Feldman: 'If he doesn't answer these questions it would be a
total cop-out. People would ask themselves, if he is truly
innocent why would he not defend himself openly by
giving straight answers to straight questions?'

Towards the end of January, a week after the giant
earthquake devastated Los Angeles, Michael Jackson
received the first bit of real good news he had had for six
months – six months which had seen him crippled both
personally and professionally. Jordan Chandler had
decided to stop his multi-million-pound civil lawsuit, after
agreeing to a financial settlement. Jackson could at last
breathe a sigh of relief – the boy's allegations of sexual
abuse had finally been silenced. But there was a high price
to pay for this silence. Exactly how much Michael Jackson
had paid to get the civil suit dropped was never revealed,
but there were many rumours: some said £3 million,
others £7 million, others £15 million, my own sources said
as much as £30 million. But one thing was sure: part of
Jackson's nightmare was over.

On 25 January at a news conference outside Santa
Monica's town hall, which lies about thirty miles from the

heart of Los Angeles, three lawyers gathered on a balmy afternoon before superior court judge David Rothman. They revealed that the singer had made a financial settlement on Jordan Chandler. Jordan's lawyer, Larry Feldman, stated: 'Both parties have agreed that the lawsuit should be resolved. It will be withdrawn in the near future.' He said that his client wanted to 'heal' and to 'put this matter behind him'. Michael Jackson's lawyer, Johnnie Cochrane, confirmed the deal but, despite the financial settlement, insisted: 'Michael Jackson is an innocent man who does not intend to have his life destroyed by rumours and innuendo.'

Only twenty-four hours earlier his legal team's defence that the child abuse allegations were merely a blackmail bid had collapsed. Police said that there was absolutely no evidence that Evan Chandler had tried to blackmail Jackson. Los Angeles deputy district attorney Michael Montagna revealed that lawyers could find no evidence of extortion despite an exhaustive probe.

One of the reasons a settlement was agreed upon, said sources close to the investigation, was because Jackson's advisers feared that the information discovered during the civil investigation would be used by prosecutors in the criminal investigation and, in the worst scenario, could even land the singer in jail. It looked, at that time, as if the end of the civil suit would spare Jackson the nightmare of a criminal trial being brought against him. Los Angeles district attorney Gil Garcetti had said he still might press charges against him but, at that time, he would not have had much of a case: under Californian law minors could not be compelled to testify and, after accepting Jackson's settlement, Chandler would not agree to do so. He was still the most important witness the police had come up with in their long and arduous investigation into the allegations against Jackson. Without Chandler, the district attorney's acting head, Lauren Weiss, admitted, the case was almost unwinnable. Los Angeles law professor Peter Arnella added: 'Without the victim there can be no criminal conclusion.'

However, the matter was not clear-cut. Some people said that the settlement would stem the flow of evidence unearthed during the civil investigation, while others said that the evidence could in fact be used if a criminal case was brought. And it was said that Jordan Chandler's evidence could still be used even if he was unwilling to appear.

And the evidence unearthed by Feldman and his team was coming in fast and furiously. A series of developments by them over the last few weeks leading up to the settlement had caused Jackson much anxiety. Feldman had taken some potentially explosive statements from key witnesses, and the former manager of Jackson's Neverland estate, Mark Quindoy, said he was ready to testify that he had seen Jackson molesting children. There was more to come. Feldman's thorough investigations were discovering many potentially damaging facts, and depositions from people such as LaToya, Jackson's former bodyguard, Marlon Brando's son Miko, and numerous other ex-employees were also looming on the horizon. Jackson himself had been ordered by the judge in the civil case to make a deposition no later than the first of February.

Another worry in the Jackson camp were the photos that the police had taken of the singer's private parts. It was said that attorney Howard Weitzman had filed a secret motion to keep the photos from being used as evidence in the criminal investigation. But Feldman wouldn't be put off, and was making things even more difficult by placing a court motion to get the intimate photographs into the public domain.

I was told by one of my sources that Jackson was terrified of going in the witness stand because he didn't want to undergo any more probing questions about the affair:

He was in for all kinds of aggressive questioning and all kinds of potential embarrassments – Larry Feldman's team had demanded a body search with pictures. By accepting this agreement Jordan would get more money than he would have, had he won the civil case. Jackson isn't worried about all the money he has shelled out. He's got a billion dollars. What he is afraid of is, his huge empire crumbling at every corner.

Before the settlement was reached there were a number of secret meetings between the two opposing legal teams and an avalanche of demands and counter demands. Originally, it was said, Jackson offered the boy $20 million (£13.5 million) spread over ten years (half the amount that Chandler was suing Jackson for). The figure was gradually raised until the sum settled was in the region of $45 million (£30 million), according to insiders who had seen the original documents.

LaToya reaffirmed this figure – in fact she slightly boosted it to $50 million (£34 million) when she appeared on American TV. She said in an interview for 'Inside Edition': 'To my understanding the little boy gets $5 million every year for the next ten years. I think it is a bad mistake on my brother's part because it shows guilt, because you're buying someone off. Michael has done that a lot. My family has done that a lot. They will buy people off in a minute.'

LaToya also reiterated the allegation that she made in Tel Aviv in December, saying that she had seen cheques made out for large amounts and she urged her brother to get help. Just a few hours after the settlement was agreed an American newspaper carried a report that the agreed figure was only $5 million. Sources close to the case believe it was planted by Jackson's team, again spreading what was seen as 'disinformation' in the hope that, if the settlement figure divulged to the media was relatively small, fans would believe that the superstar was innocent and was just paying out for what had become an irritating nuisance to him. One of the sources said: 'They do not want the large figure to be reported because many people would see an astronomical sum such as that as admission of guilt or as an admission that he has something very damaging to hide.' The total sum of the settlement was said to be around £50 million, when the legal charges for both teams of lawyers were taken into account.

The settlement apparently included agreements that neither the boy nor his family could ever talk publicly about Jackson, and some reports claimed that part of the deal was that Jordan should move out of California. Another condition imposed was that Jackson should have psychological treatment. The TV show, 'Hard Copy', whose reporter Diane Dimond had done much to uncover the news about the case, reported: 'Michael has to undergo counselling. It was a primary condition for Chandler to settle.'

The financial settlement took one more bizarre turn when it was revealed that Jackson had wanted his insurance company to pay the money agreed in the settlement. He believed that his personal liability policy with Transamerican Insurance Group would cover part of the settlement and the legal cost involved. Jackson's lawyer, Johnnie Cochran, even threatened to sue the insurance company 'for a host of claims' at one stage if it did not help the singer.

To many people, the deal showed that Jackson was guilty and was buying the boy's silence. The out-of-court settlement exposed Jackson straight away to charges of having paid hush money. To others, it demonstrated the power of money. New York lawyer Raoul Felder, who has been involved in many high-profile cases, said: 'The settlement is disgusting. It sends a message to America that if you're rich and famous, you can throw a little of your gold at the scales of justice until they tip your way. It is saying that if you're rich you can abuse children. Also I think if you're innocent you don't give someone millions.'

Laurie Levensen, a criminal law professor in Los Angeles, concurred: 'The perception is if you have a lot of money, you can buy your way out of trouble.' Even a fan commented: 'If Michael is so innocent, I don't think he should have settled. If anything it makes him look guilty.'

Elton John, who helped Jackson while he was being treated for drug addiction, said if he had been in Jackson's shoes he would never have given in. Elton added: 'I wouldn't have settled. I wouldn't care if I had to sell the last thing in my life, just to clear my name, that's what I would have done.'

Before the deal was agreed a number of distinguished lawyers said a settlement would harm Jackson. Marvyn Kornberg, a lawyer in the Long Island 'Lolita' trial who represents Joey Buttafuco, told New York's *Daily News*: 'It would be suicidal for Michael Jackson to settle civilly while there is a pending criminal case against him. The DA can still subpoena the boy and there is no way they can keep the records from him – you can't withhold evidence.' While lawyer Eric Naiberg, who represents Long Island 'Lolita', Amy Fisher, added: 'If there was a settlement, it could hurt his criminal case.'

The public reaction to Jackson's settlement did not bode well for him at first. In a poll conducted jointly by America's national paper, *USA Today*, and the global cable news channel, CNN, more than half of the people polled (55 per cent) said that the settlement made the singer look guilty, while 59 per cent thought Jackson should have fought the charges and not backed down; only 23 per cent thought that he should have made a settlement. Nevertheless, a huge 69 per cent of pollsters felt that he should carry on with his career.

The settlement was a complete about-turn by Jackson's legal team who had said on numerous occasions that there would be no settlement whatsoever. It was also curious that the star's legal team were now paying out *more* than Chandler had supposedly demanded in his alleged blackmail attempt.

Sources close to Jackson said that he wanted a quick solution to the nightmare that was threatening to ruin his career, and that a settlement was, in the end, the only way out. To Jackson, whatever the price, it was money well spent. He saw it as a way of avoiding an extremely public trial, which would have been televised to every corner of the world.

Jordan Chandler's lawyer denied any charges of hush money, saying that the young boy was also agreeing to this deal to 'finally get some peace':

I have done what is in this little boy's interest. He has an enormous amount of courage and we are both very happy with the resolution. We've been at this for six months. That's a long time for anybody. For a child it is an eternity. We've done this so the boy can gain peace and be able to repair very deep wounds. He gets to play out with his friends now and can turn on the TV without seeing himself in the news.

Despite the settlement, police pressed ahead with the criminal investigation and were still questioning potential witnesses. A day after the settlement it was reported that they had lined up a second investigation to replace the Chandler one. The boy at the centre of this investigation had not been named, but he had been interviewed for hours shortly following the news that Jordan Chandler had been paid millions to drop his lawsuit.

Over the last few months, however, the police have

found that much of the potential evidence against the
singer has been drying up. It was as if their every lead
was being thwarted. Numerous people, who expressed an
initial willingness, never actually appeared in court. But
top private investigator Sandra Sutherland, who worked
for Larry Feldman, stressed that Jordan Chandler's family
and legal team decided to drop the case primarily to stop
the young man being forced to endure a harrowing and
painful court ordeal.

My Los Angeles sources told me, as rumours of the
settlement began to appear: 'The settlement is for $45 mil-
lion. The agreement has been ironed out for the last few
weeks. And though people are saying it is over ten years,
I'm not sure. I have heard that it is going to be quicker.
One of the terms of the settlement is that Jordan should
move out of California.'

At the beginning of February the battle between
Michael Jackson and LaToya erupted into open warfare.
The singer was apparently set to launch a multi-million-
pound lawsuit against her in a bid to silence more allegations about his sex life. The reports said that LaToya was
planning to claim that Jackson has sexually abused at least
thirty boys and that he was paying for many of them
to have psychiatric counselling. 'Some of the boys will
never be normal again,' she said. 'It's so heart-breaking
to think of the lives that have been ruined because of my
brother's perversion.' In a counter-attack, it was said
that Jackson had instructed his lawyers to sue his sister
for defamation of character and was also planning to leak
some sensational secrets about her. It was believed that
Jackson had been persuaded to go on the attack as part
of a carefully orchestrated plan to restore his image and
reputation.

LaToya hit back by saying that she would also launch
a lawsuit against her brother if he carried out his threat
to sue her. Her manager-husband said: 'Let him sue.

We'll take him to court for one billion dollars for malicious prosecution and a series of very serious undisclosed counts.'

A week after these reports, a grand jury in Santa Barbara began hearing evidence against Jackson. The district attorney decided to go ahead with the hearing despite the singer's £30 million payout. The secret hearing was to decide if the star should be criminally charged with abusing Jordan Chandler. Early on in the hearing Jackson's personal assistant, Norma Staikos, refused to answer a single question about the child abuse claims when she faced the grand jury. Staikos, who worked for the singer for eight years and organized his diary, pleaded the fifth amendment, which allows witnesses to refuse to give evidence which might incriminate them.

The decision to convene the grand jury indicated that the criminal investigation had not been halted. And there was even concern in the Jackson camp that Jordan Chandler might indeed be forced to testify in a criminal case. Los Angeles prosecutor Gil Garcetti was backing a new law which will make sex abuse victims give evidence even if they have been paid 'hush money'.

Towards the end of March it was reported that prosecutors trying to build the child abuse case against the singer had made a breakthrough and that two boys – and one of their mother's – had agreed to give evidence against Jackson to the grand jury which had been set up to see if the singer would be charged. One of the investigators said of the trio – who were all in protective custody in safe houses – 'They are key and crucial witnesses. We believe their evidence will be explosive and very damaging to Jackson. There is no question in my mind that charges could be brought against the singer.'

One of the boys, from Southern California, claims to have been abused several years ago, while the other boy and his mother have told investigators that he was a victim of Jackson's sexual appetite. Another source commented: 'The mother has also told police that she witnessed a number of suspicious events. She has agreed to give chapter and verse.' Police were also said to have been talking to the son of a famous actress, whom they believe could have been a victim of abuse, and were planning to interview child actor Macaulay Culkin again.

Up till these revelations, most of those called before the Santa Barbara grand jury had been on Jackson's side. These included actor Marlon Brando's 33-year-old son Miko, who once worked for Jackson and Jackson's former assistant Norma Staikos. One frustrated investigator admitted: 'Most of the people up before the jury have been hostile witness. They haven't co-operated with the police.'

A few weeks later rumours emerged that police were to drop the case against Michael Jackson and that the singer's ordeal was over. Private investigator Don Crutchfield, who lists Marlon Brando among his clients, told the American TV programme 'Hard Copy' that the police investigation, which had lasted seven months, was now finished. He claimed that district attorneys' offices in both Los Angeles and Santa Barbara had tagged the singer's files as 'DA Rejects', adding: 'It was a case where money talked. The boy was paid off. When he refused to testify, there was no case.' 'Hard Copy' reporter Diane Dimond also confirmed that there would be no police charges and it was unlikely that a court case would be brought against Jackson. She admitted: 'The police are not going to seek an indictment. The decision was made a long time ago, but they allowed the grand jury to carry on sitting.'

But the following day Los Angeles district attorney Gil Garcetti and his Santa Barbara counterpart Tom Sneddon attacked the reports that the case had been dropped because neither Jordan Chandler nor Jackson's camp were willing to testify amid allegations that witnesses had been intimidated by the singer's top aides. Sneddon said: 'There have been rumours that this case is to be rejected. I would categorically like to deny that. The grand jury currently in session has been extended.' A superior court judge prolonged the jury's sessions, which were originally due to last ninety days, so that prosecutors could be given more time to produce evidence.

Michael Jackson's millions of fans all over the world protested loudly and constantly about his innocence. But there was one fan who took it further than most and it ended up with her being imprisoned in a Los Angeles jail. Pretty blonde-haired Denise Pfeiffer, from Leicestershire, was alleged to have been hounding Jordan Chandler's family and waging a campaign of hate and terror against them, details of which the police say they found in her diary.

On 12 April, Denise, described by many of her friends as Jackson's number one fan, was brought into the Beverly Hills Municipal Court. There she was accused of spray-painting an obscene message outside Evan Chandler's dental practice, leaving a threatening message on his answering machine and stealing the keys to his office toilet. Pfeiffer, who was wearing orange prison clothes with her hands manacled behind her back, denied all the charges, but as she was unable to raise the $10,000 bail she was remanded in custody until her trial.

Denise, who could face twenty years in jail if found guilty, has devoted her life to Michael Jackson for the last twelve years. The police say she was intent on tracking down Jordan and his family because she believed they lied to extort money and to try to destroy her idol. She was found inside the Chandlers' new family home by Jordan's stepmother on Thursday 7 April, who with the help of another relative kept her there until police arrived and arrested her. Police claim Pfeiffer, who is said to suffer from anorexia, flew to America two months ago to track down the family.

Denise, who spent £10,000 following Michael Jackson's *Dangerous* tour around the world and flew to Las Vegas to see Jackson's first singing appearance since the civil lawsuit was settled, denies she was stalking Jordan, his father or the rest of his family. Speaking from prison, she said:

> I can't believe this is happening to me. All I did was make a few phone calls telling them to stop lying about Michael and went to their new house. I just wanted to scare them into telling the truth and end all the lies they have been telling. But I am desperate in here. My life is not worth living any more and I just want to die. If Michael hears about this I might just as well kill myself.

But Denise was rescued from her prison ordeal by a good fairy in the shape of British actress Lynn Redgrave, who lives in America, and who put up the $10,000 bail money after hearing of the young woman's plight. Denise, who spent six days in the city's notorious county prison before being freed, was overjoyed when the actress came to her aid.

Lynn, explaining why she had put up the large amount of bail, said: 'Stars wouldn't be where they are if it wasn't for fans. I thought it was wrong that she should be locked up.'

Jackson did not make the first payment of his settlement with Jordan Chandler until almost three months had elapsed from the original deal. The cheque, which was for $1,850,755 (£1.3 million) was drawn from the singer's personal account at the City National Bank on 24 March after it was said that Larry Feldman had given Jackson a 5 p.m deadline on that day because he was worried that no money was forthcoming. Six days later, on 30 March, a second cheque for $2.8 million (almost £2 million) was drawn on the same account for Jordan.

It was believed that Jackson's aides had withheld the money because they wanted to be sure that Jordan Chandler would not testify against Jackson in the police prosecution – but now with the young boy already getting over $4 million police prosecutors had resigned themselves to the fact that the boy, who for a long time had been their hope as their star witness, would never testify against the singer he claimed had persistently abused him.

A source told *Today* newspaper:

Jackson's attorneys have been watching the criminal case develop closely. They were initially alarmed by the police's determination to press ahead once the civil case had been settled. They knew there was no point in paying off the boy if he was going to give evidence which could put Jackson behind bars, so they withheld payment. Larry Feldman was getting uneasy and finally gave an ultimatum that if no money was forthcoming by 5 p.m. on 24 March he would take further action. Once Jackson's attorneys were convinced a conviction hinged on Jordy's full co-operation, and they were satisfied he wouldn't testify, they paid.

Nevertheless, police were still pressing ahead with their investigations and in mid-April it was revealed that they wanted to examine seven locked vaults containing videos at the Warner Brothers studios, which they believe could harbour some of Jackson's most personal possessions.

A police source said: 'Our investigation will continue. We will not stop until we are satisfied that we have examined all the evidence. Only then will it be determined whether to bring criminal charges against Michael Jackson.'

CHAPTER 11

The Future

MICHAEL JACKSON'S SINGING COMEBACK was not the spectacular success that would have been the perfect fairy-tale ending to the months of nightmare he had endured. In many ways it was an anticlimax, and several of the fans, who had paid up to £675 to see the star perform, booed and jeered him. Many felt that Jackson had let them down when he appeared on stage and sang just twenty words.

The concert was held in Las Vegas on Saturday, 19 February. It was billed as 'The Jackson Family Honours', the ultimate showbiz reunion: the entire Jackson family would appear together on stage for the first time in twenty years. The faithful fans were expecting a feast of entertainment. A few guest stars performed live, but much of the show was taken up by videos. Jackson only joined his family on stage for a final song, 'If You Only Believe'. Then he addressed the crowd: 'Thank you for your prayers. Thank you for your loyalty. Thank you for your love and your friendship.'

But some of the audience there were furious they had paid a fortune just to see the star for a few minutes. It was then that Jackson's friend Liz Taylor, upset and angry, walked on stage and silenced the jeering crowd: 'Stop that, it's not nice,' she said to them. 'Don't boo. That's an ugly sound.' She explained that Jackson could not sing for them because he had nothing prepared to sing. During her introductory speech, Taylor had tried to ease the singer's nervousness in this, his first stage appearance since the scandal had blown up in his face the previous August, by saying:

> Michael, we who know you better than others acknowledge the suffering you have endured because we have suffered with you too. In the midst of our deepest anguish we had no doubt that you would prevail in these darkest hours and you emerged – still innocent, still trusting, magical, untouched by the tongues and opinions of the world. Michael, we know that your recent torture is not going to change your compassion for children. Surely, Michael, you are still the king of pop without a doubt.

Jermaine Jackson, who co-produced the show, also defended his brother's short appearance. He said: 'This is not a Michael Jackson show. This is the Jackson Family Honours. This is a charity event intended to help the less fortunate.'

It was said the high price of the tickets put many fans off. More than 3,000 out of the 15,000 seats were left unsold, even though tickets had been drastically reduced forty-eight hours before the concert. Originally LaToya Jackson was to be part of the show, but she declined to appear at all and instead held court at a nearby hotel, offering interviews to the media. She claimed: 'They wanted me to sign these papers meaning that I had to say nothing about Michael and I refused.'

In the wake of all the worldwide publicity there has been about Michael Jackson, many psychologists have taken an interest in his case. Dr Glenn D. Wilson, a senior lecturer in psychology at the Institute of Psychiatry at the University of London, believes that one of the key triggers to

Michael Jackson's behaviour is his deep-rooted desire for youth:

> Jackson does seem fixated on the idea of youth in himself as well as others. Clearly he is fascinated by children and obsessed with the idea of retaining youthful looks. Surrounding himself with young people might well be seen as an extension of that obsession.
>
> It's obvious that he's had a lot of cosmetic surgery which is intended to keep him looking young, youthful and androgynous to some extent. And it's a characteristic of pre-pubescent children that they are androgynous – before puberty little boys are much more like little girls. He seems somewhat obsessed by that phase of development and doesn't want to leave it behind him. It seems to have extended to his companions. And surrounding himself not only with children but with all kinds of childish props such as fun fairs and video games is another way of hanging on to a childhood which he feels is eluding him.
>
> Another possibility is that he is fixated on the time when he was the youngest member of the Jackson Five and doesn't want to relinquish that role as the youngster who was appealling because he was so cute. Coupled with that could be the interpretation that Jackson had such a good time and so much attention lavished on him as a child that he doesn't want to leave that phase of his life behind him.

On the wider subject of paedophilia, Dr Wilson, who has written a book about the psychology of show business called *Psychology for Performing Artists: Butterflies and Bouquets* which was published in February, says:

Paedophiles are often people who feel threatened by adults to the extent that they don't feel they can approach them for sexual favours. They need something extremely submissive and innocent. Given that they have a gay orientation in the first place thereafter they go for everything which is effeminate, submissive or female in the male partner. Moving towards very young partners is a way of rendering them more female.

Homosexual play between pubescent peers is quite common, for example public school boys play with each other in the normal stage of development. If Jackson is indeed frozen at that stage of pubescent development then that kind of homosexual play would not be pathological or out of order. He may have just deceived himself that he is that young. It's possible that he has certain mental characteristics of a child – general immaturity such that he identifies with being a child and prefers to act as one.

However, Wilson believes it was naive of Jackson to think that his love of children would not be turned against him:

One of the big pressures on performers is the loss of privacy. In the case of someone like Michael Jackson he can't make a move without the fear of it being reported.

It could be that some of the boys or their parents saw Jackson's fondness for childhood or children as an opportunity – they might have encouraged their links in the first place because he is such a celebrity and then somewhere along the line they have figured his behaviour is out of order and they chose to get him on this. It could even be that perhaps he did them wrong so they went for revenge or they thought they saw an opportunity for mega-bucks.

One of the great difficulties of being a pop star, apart from the lack of privacy, is suspicion of those about you. You are never quite sure of their motives. You have a wealth of fans approaching you, including people who want favours from you – groupies are an obvious example – and it is difficult to know who your friends are. If some youngster approaches Jackson, he doesn't know if they are genuinely fond of him or if they are going to capitalize on it in some way. For that reason a number of stars shy away from relationships though others use it to their advantage.

The danger of Jackson settling out of court is that a lot more people may start to demand more money. When he appeared in front of the cameras to proclaim his innocence he sounded like a sad and broken man. You get the feeling that he needs a long rest. It's not to say he can't come back, but he will need all the help he can get to do it. He is a very shy almost puritannical person and he will need a break from the public eye. I would say he is almost certainly in some kind of therapy and with his money he can afford the best. Jackson will now feel very wary of whom he associates himself with.

He has shown every indication of being a vulnerable person. It is difficult to predict what will happen, but I'd say he has a real uphill fight on his hands and it won't be easy for him. It will probably take him at least six months to get himself together again.

American psychiatrist Dr Carole Lieberman, who has made a detailed study of the singer, believes Jackson is innocent. But she is of the opinion that his personal growth – both pyschological and sexual – has been stunted because of what happened to him in childhood.

She says:

I think the psychological traumas that Jackson suffered as a child have been such that they have not allowed him to function as an adult male on a psycho-sexual level. There were many traumas, but in particular he was exposed at a very young age to his father's infidelities and his father's cavalier attitude to sex, which actually had an effect on all the brothers to some degree. But because he was the youngest one on the road when they travelled he was most affected by it.

Since many of the incidents occurred during the early days of development when a young boy would be rivalling his father for his mother's affections, they had a greater impact. He was torn between not displeasing his father so that he would not be thrown out of the band, but then being forced to betray his mother whose affections he desired more than anybody.

He would have been exposed to a lot of blatant sexuality through performing in clubs where there were strippers and raunchy dancers, so that sex from an early age became something that was confusing and terrifying to him.

Lieberman believes Jackson is attracted to children because he doesn't have faith in adults:

Jackson surrounds himself with children because he can trust children and everyone else in the world he can't trust. He learnt from an early age to be afraid of trusting people. He learnt that the only people one could trust were children who had not been corrupted by an adult world. The Neverland ranch is the clearest example of how he identifies with Peter Pan.

He says that he likes to be with children to live

the childhood he never had and that is part of it, too. He likes the idea of making children happy because that helps him make up for his own lack of happiness in his own childhood. By being in a sense the parent that he never had he can in some ways make up for what he lacked during childhood.

Jackson may have been naive but one has to look at him in the context of him being the psychological age of a pre-pubescent boy. That would be approximately nine to twelve. It is not unusual for pre-pubescent boys to be sleeping in each other's beds and to have cetain sexual exploratory behaviour. I do not think he is guilty of child molestation and if indeed there were any behaviour such as touching, hugging or even taking baths together, that would come under normal behaviour for a pre-pubescent child.

Lieberman is concerned about Jackson's health:

I think Jackson is now in a very fragile state. I think he is still in denial as to how much the allegations and the media circus have impacted on him.

I think his genius is his sensitivity. It not only makes him fragile psychologically but it also makes him a creative genius. He is at one with the music he makes, and he is only able to do that by using the creativity that comes out of being such a sensitive soul.

It would be very difficult for him to be creative at the moment. Sometimes people can be quite creative out of their pain, but if their pain is overwhelming it can interfere with the creative process. I think things will be difficult until there is a sense of closure about everything.

Lieberman is of the opinion that many people want to believe the accusations because they are envious of everything Jackson has achieved. She says:

> I think in America our society likes to build people up into idols that cannot possibly be as perfect as the public wants them to be. What happens is that the public gets jealous of their fame, money and power. In order to take the power back, they take delight in tearing them down. I would say that the majority of health professionals are quick to presume he is guilty, like so many of the public do. These are, however, people who on the whole know very little of his background. They know what they read in the papers and see on TV and that is it.

Lieberman believes Jackson should seek therapy immediately and concludes:

> Jackson is unable to cause harm, true harm to another child. I believe he is incapable of that. For someone who has done so much for children, the allegations would be all the more traumatic because he would have felt even more misunderstood and less appreciated.

So what of the future? Once upon a time scandals did and could destroy celebrities. The one that has been cited often as the Michael Jackson scenario unfolded is the case of Fatty Arbuckle. Arbuckle was one of Hollywood's biggest stars in the 1920s; his silent comedies made him box office magic. But his world of mirth caved in on him when he was tried for murder: a beautiful starlet, Victoria Rappe, died after he allegedly raped her during a wild party. Though Arbuckle was found innocent, his career was ruined and he died a broken man. But that was in the

1920s when moral and religious attitudes were much sterner than they are now. Since the liberation that came with the sixties, all kinds of celebrities – from presidents down – have been embroiled in scandals; most have survived. And there have been plenty of other show-business scandals. Roman Polanski was accused of seducing a fifteen-year-old girl, and Woody Allen became his own step-daughter's lover. Neither of their careers was damaged.

But Michael Jackson's scandal involves uncomfortable issues: the public are naturally very hostile towards child sex abuse and homosexual paedophilia. If only, people say, he could have got involved with a twenty-two-year-old homosexual actor or become Diana Ross's toy-boy, the scandal could have been accepted. Jackson's involvement and love of children, and the money he donated to children's' charities, somehow only makes the whole scandal worse. His love for children has been tainted, and even a charity that he was involved in sued him for fraud. As a role model for children, he is no longer credible.

Certainly it looks as if most sponsorship organizations will no longer be willing to throw their dollars behind Jackson with the abandon they once showed. His biggest sponsors, Pepsi-Cola, dropped their endorsement deal within weeks of the allegations being made. His record company, Sony, seemed most economical with their support in the months before the settlement was finally reached. They issued the briefest of statements: 'We continue to stay in contact with Michael Jackson and his management. For Sony Music to comment any further would not be appropriate except to stand by the right that even a superstar is innocent until proven guilty.' Jo Smith, a music consultant, told the *Wall Street Journal*: 'God knows when Sony will get a record out of the guy again. He's very fragile emotionally and even under the best circumstances he only delivers an album every couple of years.'

There is no doubt that Jackson, despite being emotionally shattered by his ordeal, will still go on making magical records, records that the world will rush out and buy. But will he still remain the world's number one superstar – the cultural phenomenon whose name is recognized from Sri Lanka to Siberia? It will be a long, hard struggle for Jackson, but he is someone who knows all about struggle – his whole life has been a fight to become the greatest performer the world has ever seen. He has never been interested in being second best.

If Jackson ever decides that the battle to get back to the top of the pop heap is too arduous, he knows there is one place where he can escape from the allegations and rumours that have plagued and worn him down over the last year. It is a remote place on Africa's Ivory Coast called Krindjab, where the Agni tribe live. Jackson visited the faraway place two years ago, and there he was treated like royalty as he was carried and paraded through its poor streets. An emissary from the king told the singer at the height of the scandal, when things looked far bleaker for him than they do now: 'Our doors are always open. Our home is your home, to our tribe you are the King of Sani, a man of dignity and honour.'

THE BAD YEAR CHRONOLOGY

JANUARY

19 Jackson performs at an Inaugural gala for President Bill Clinton at the White House.

31 Jackson performs during half-time at the Super Bowl and 91 million people tune in.

FEBRUARY

10 Jackson does his first proper TV interview for fourteen years with America's top chat host Oprah Winfrey. Their ninety-minute encounter is broadcast live from Michael's 2,700 acre ranch Neverland in Santa Barbara and is watched by hundreds of millions of people around the world, including 62 million in America and 11.5 million in Britain. He tells her he is romancing Brooke Shields.

12 The star invites thirteen-year-old Jordan, his half-sister Lily and their mother June to Neverland. It is their first ever visit.

18 Actress Brooke Shields denies any romance between herself and Jackson. She says they are just good friends.

24 Jackson appears at the Grammy awards with his sister Janet.

MARCH

9 Jackson performs at the Soul Train Music Awards from a wheelchair after spraining his ankle. He wins awards for the best album, *Dangerous*, and the best R&B single, 'Remember The Time'.

28 Jackson takes Jordan Chandler, his half-sister Lily
and his mother June to Las Vegas. It is here, Jordan
later claims, that Jackson spends his first night in
bed with him.

MAY
Jackson takes his new 'family' to Monte Carlo
where he receives three awards at the World Music
Awards. At the end of the evening a fan lunges at
him and he is rescued by bodyguards.

JUNE
13 Jackson launches his new MJJ/Epic record label
with the soundtrack from the movie *Free Willy*.

AUGUST
4 A meeting takes place between Evan Chandler,
Jackson and the singer's private detective Anthony
Pellicano. Pellicano later claims that during the
meeting Chandler demanded a £13-million pay-off.
The deal involved Jackson setting up Chandler as a
Hollywood screenwriter with a £3.25 million 'salary'
over four years.

5 Pellicano offers Evan Chandler £230,000 as a film
development deal. Pellicano later says he was trying
to set up Chandler with extortion and that the offer
did not suggest in any way that the sex abuse
allegations were true.

16 Evan Chandler's lawyers are served with papers for
him to produce his son Jordan in court so he can be
handed back to his mother after she sued her ex-
husband for custody.

17 Evan Chandler takes Jordan to therapist Dr Mathis
Abrams, who reports the boy's allegations of child
abuse to the Los Angeles police. The LAPD launch
a criminal investigation into the singer. Evan

Chandler obtains a court ruling which stops Jackson having any contact with his son.

21   Los Angeles police armed with a search warrant raid Jackson's Neverland ranch in Santa Barbara and his secret apartment in Century City, Los Angeles.

22   Jackson leaves America for Bangkok, Thailand, where he is to launch the second leg of his *Dangerous* tour.

23   Jackson is named in the child abuse police investigation. Police confirm they have raided his Neverland home and formally announce their investigation of the singer.

24   Jackson issues a brief statement through his lawyer Howard Weitzman to refute the allegations. Anthony Pellicano claims that Jackson was the victim of a woman's unsuccessful extortion attempt.

Jackson plays his first show in Bangkok to 40,000 ecstatic fans.

25   Jordan Chandler's claims that Jackson made him take part in sex acts are leaked.

Jackson pulls out of his second Bangkok show just three hours before he is due to go on stage. Tour doctor Stuart Finkelstein says the singer was suffering from acute dehydration because of the city's heat and humidity.

26   Two of Jackson's young pals, Brett Barnes and Wade Robson, confess that they shared a bed with the star but that no sex took place.

Jackson cancels his Bangkok concert for the second time, fuelling rumours that he is sick with worry over the scandal. He issues a statement urging his fans to stay calm and promising he will perform on 27 August.

The Jackson camp denies the star has tried to commit suicide.

27   Jackson gives his concert in Bangkok.

Jordan Chandler's full allegations are revealed, contained in a report of an interview with Jordan by staff of the Los Angeles Department of Children's Services.

Jack Gordon claims that his wife LaToya warned Jackson to end his friendships with young boys five months ago. Gordon says that he and his wife are worried that Jackson may crack under the strain.

28 Jackson flies from Bangkok to Singapore. He arrives at the city's Raffles Hotel in a van with the curtains drawn to a warm welcome from hundreds of fans.

Liz Taylor also jets into Singapore to be with Jackson on his birthday.

Jackson's lawyer Howard Weitzman claims that Evan Chandler is being investigated by the Los Angeles police for blackmail.

29 Michael Jackson celebrates his 35th birthday with a spectacular show in front of 45,000 screaming fans at Singapore's National Stadium. The audience sing 'Happy Birthday' to him and cry out 'We love you!' during the show.

Evan Chandler claims he was offered hush-money to put a stop to his son's allegations against Jackson. Anthony Pellicano acknowledges that June Schwartz knew nothing about any blackmail attempts or anything about her son's alleged abuse.

Pepsi-Cola say they have launched an internal inquiry into Jackson's private life.

British disc jockey Terry George alleges that Jackson made an obscene phone call to him when he was a thirteen-year-old schoolboy.

Cliff Richard defends Jackson, saying: 'Michael Jackson is probably the best singer in the world today, but when you become a public image you are up for grabs and you are very vulnerable.'

30   Jackson's family hold a press conference in Los
         Angeles to declare their love and total support for the
         singer.

         It is revealed that five children named by Jordan
         Chandler as fellow victims told investigators that
         Jackson never molested them.

         Jackson's star on the Hollywood Walk Of Fame
         on Hollywood Boulevard has been transformed into
         a shrine where fans gather to place flowers, pray
         and pledge their support for the singer.

         Jackson falls ill, collapsing in his dressing-room
         minutes before he is due to take the stage in
         Singapore. It is the third cancellation of a show –
         the third in six days – since the child abuse allegations
         erupted.

         A secretly taped phone call is played on American
         TV in which Evan Chandler describes Jackson as an
         'evil guy' and in which he claims he has evidence
         against him that will prevent him ever selling another
         record.

31   Jackson is given the all-clear after a brain scan at
         Singapore's Mount Victoria Hospital.

SEPTEMBER

2   Jordan Chandler's lawyer Gloria Allred says her
         young client is looking forward to testifying against
         Jackson in court. Says Allred: 'The boy is absolutely
         devastated by what happened and wants the truth to
         come out.'

3   Jackson's parents hold an emotional news
         conference in Taipei, Taiwan, in another public show
         of support for their son.

         Actress Sharon Stone attacks the Chandler family.
         Speaking at the MTV Music Awards, she says: 'I
         believe that if this boy's family has, or ever had,
         evidence of abuse then it would have surfaced by

now. All I know is that if a child of mine had been abused, I would not have been making deals.'

4 Jackson's four siblings fly to Taiwan, where the singer gives the first of his two concerts.

5 Jackson's former estate manager at Neverland, Mark Quindoy, claims he watched the singer put his hand in a nine-year-old boy's pants as they sat by a jacuzzi. He is also reported to have seen Jackson kiss a seven-year-old on the lips.

Jackson goes on a spending spree as a Taiwan store opens up specially for him for two hours. He spends around £3,000 on toys and videos.

6 LaToya claims that Jackson was betrayed by one of his workers who set him up on sexual molestation charges.

7 Jackson arrives in Fukuoka, Japan, amidst rumours that he may have to break off his tour to return to America within the next few days to face police investigators.

9 Jackson drops out of a deal to write a theme song for the upcoming film *Addams Family Values*.

12 Jordan Chandler's lawyer Gloria Allred quits after a bitter row over the way she wants to handle the case.

Jackson arrives in Moscow.

14 Jordan Chandler hits Jackson with a multi-million-pound civil lawsuit. The seventeen-page suit, case No. SCO2622 filed at Santa Monica Superior Court, charges the singer with sexual battery, seduction, wilful misconduct, fraud and negligence.

15 Michael Jackson plays Moscow, his first ever concert in Russia.

17 It is reported that lawyers for Jordan Chandler plan to serve Jackson with a subpoena demanding that he return to Los Angeles next month to be cross-examined.

Jackson arrives in Israel for his two concerts a day

late after his flight from Moscow is delayed by bad
weather. He is met by thousands of fans at Tel Aviv's
Ben-Gurion airport where he is presented with
apples and honey — symbols of the Jewish New Year
— by an eight-year-old girl.

18   Hundreds of fans mob the star when he visits one
of the holiest places in the world, Jerusalem's Wailing
Wall. Worshippers at the Wall are furious and
accuse Jackson of desecrating the Sabbath. He is
prevented from going through the Wall as
worshippers bar his way.

19   Jackson plays his first show in Tel Aviv. It is Israel's
largest ever rock concert.

22   Police fly over 7,000 miles to Manila in the
Philippines to interview Mark and Faye Quindoy. The
couple gave the police the names of four young boys
that Jackson was particularly intimate with. Mark
Quindoy stated: 'I saw Michael fondling, kissing and
molesting other children. I left his employ because I
couldn't stand it any more.'

23   Jackson cancels two shows in South Africa blaming
the country's political violence.

27   Jackson cancels three shows in Australia — 3, 4 and
7 December — amid speculation that he is about to
return home to face cross-examination about the
child abuse allegations.

28   Jackson arrives at Liz Taylor's luxury chalet in
Gstaad, Switzerland, for a short break. He spends a
few days there with two young boy pals Eddie and
Frank Cascio, aged nine and thirteen, and their
father.

OCTOBER

9   Jackson greets photographers besieging his hotel in
Buenos Aires, Argentina, by holding up a copy of
Child magazine from his balcony.

11   Jackson is warned by his aides that he could be arrested when he returns to America. It is reported that police have enough evidence to recommend charging the singer.

14   The singer wins a ten-day reprieve in answering the civil law suit brought against him by Jordan Chandler after his lawyers claim they weren't given enough time.

15   Jackson goes on a shopping trip with three young boy pals while in São Paulo, Brazil.

20   Police raid the offices of Jackson's skin specialist Arnold Klein and his plastic surgeon Steven Hoefflin and hunt through medical files, photographs and documents. The searches seem to confirm stories that Jordan Chandler has told investigators of distinguishing marks on the singer's private parts. Dr Klein is interviewed by police for more than two hours.

29   Jackson is ordered to return to America by 1 November to answer the child sex abuse allegations. If he fails to return to answer questions under oath, lawyers for Jordan Chandler could demand a court order to force him to come back.

   Jackson's Neverland ranch is threatened by massive fires sweeping across California.

30   It is reported that Jackson will ignore the deadline and continue his tour as planned.

31   Jackson is snubbed by the organizers of a star-studded party to celebrate Mickey Mouse's 65th birthday in November at a lavish bash in Florida.

NOVEMBER

1   Jackson's lawyers demand that the multi-million-pound civil suit brought by Jordan Chandler be postponed for six years because they feel that the civil proceedings could influence any future criminal case which might come about as a result of police investigations. Under US law a criminal charge must be made within six years of the alleged offence.

8 Police search the Jackson family home in Encino. Sources say they were hunting for videos and photos of nude boys in 'sexually explicit poses'.

Jackson is questioned in Mexico City by lawyers after he is accused of stealing songs from two songwriters.

10 Jackson is again grilled in Mexico over copyright infringement case.

12 Jackson scraps the remainder of his *Dangerous* tour and vanishes. His sudden decision comes after speculation that he might be arrested in Puerto Rico, where he is due to play a concert on 14 November. The island is a US dependency and loosely within US legal jurisdiction.

13 Jackson arrives at Luton airport, at 12.20 a.m. Accompanying him in the private, luxury Boeing 727 jet are Liz Taylor, her husband Larry Fortenski, Jackson's security chief Bill Bray and a number of bodyguards.

14 Pepsi-Cola drop Jackson from their campaign. Pepsi admitted: 'All links have come to an end.'

15 Jackson's lawyer Bertram Fields says Jackson is so messed up by his addiction to painkilling drugs that he is 'barely able to function on an intellectual level' and can hardly speak. It is revealed that Jackson is being treated for a 'complete emotional breakdown' by therapist Beauchamp Colclough, the man who helped save Elton John from drink and drug problems.

16 The lawyer who grilled Michael Jackson over a copyright dispute, Howard Manning, says Jackson showed no signs of being ill or of being a drug addict at breaking point. He said: 'He looked fine to me.'

18 Jackson is said to be in an incoherent daze after receiving mega doses of Valium for his painkiller addiction.

It is reported that police have found a photograph of a nude five-year-old boy in a locked briefcase in the singer's bedroom after the raid on his parent's house.

19 Los Angles' district attorney writes to Jackson's lawyers asking that the singer be given up for questioning.

20 Elizabeth Taylor admits that she has helped Jackson find treatment for his addiction.

A superior court judge orders Jackson to submit to a deposition for the civil suit before 31 January 1994.

Jackson's record company Sony say sales of *Dangerous* have exceeded 20 million worldwide.

21 There is speculation that Jackson could be in Europe to have plastic surgery on his private parts after Jordan Chandler described what they looked like to investigators.

22 Beauchamp Colclough officially confirms he is treating Michael Jackson.

23 Judge David Rothman throws out a plea by Jackson's lawyers to delay the civil action brought by Jordan Chandler for six years. He sets a date of 31 March for the start of the lawsuit. He also rejects a plea that Jackson is too ill to be interrogated under oath and says he must be questioned personally by Jordan's lawyers.

24 New court papers allege that Jackson asked a former security guard to search out and destroy a hidden Polaroid photo of a naked boy.

Jackson's lawyer Betram Fields stops working for the singer after letting it slip that he thought criminal charges against Jackson were 'imminent'.

25 It is revealed that one of Jackson's former pals, fourteen-year-old Jimmy Safechuck, has been quizzed by a grand jury in Santa Barbara for two hours.

It is also revealed that Jackson has pulled off a record-breaking £100-million music deal after switching his music publishing to record giant EMI.

26 Seven more boys, all friends of Jackson, are interviewed by police officers.

29 Former security guard Leroy Thomas claims that Jackson had as many as twenty boys spend the night with him at his parents' home, after smuggling them in. Thomas and four other security men, who are suing Jackson for unfair dismissal, claim that Jackson never had a girlfriend stay overnight and no adult friends ever visited him during the time they worked for him.

DECEMBER

1 In a deposition to Jordan Chandler's lawyers, Gary Hearne, Jackson's chauffeur, says the singer spent at least thirty nights sleeping at Jordan Chandler's home.

3 Jackson's lawyer says the star will return to America by mid-January to answer questions in the civil lawsuit against him.

6 The team of doctors who are treating Michael Jackson for his painkiller addiction say they believe he is not guilty of the child molestation charges. They say they are convinced he has never had sex with a man or woman, let alone a child.

7 America's top comedienne Roseanne Arnold launches an attack on Jackson. She says: 'When a

35-year-old man is sleeping in the same bed as little schoolboys there is something seriously wrong.'

Jackson's brother Jermaine insists that the star is innocent, saying: 'He didn't do it. The family is 1,000 per cent behind him.'

12   Jackson returns to America for the first time since the allegations and the ensuing scandal erupted. He lands in California in a private aircraft.

13   Anthony Pellicano's former assistant Gina Christian claims that her ex-boss forced Jackson's doctor to breach confidentiality and reveal Jackson's addiction to painkillers so he could buy more time for the singer. She also said that he grilled a frightened Jordan Chandler for forty-five minutes and then played the tape to four abuse therapists in a bid to prove Jordan was lying, but the four therapists all said they believed the boy's answers were honest.

EuroDisney axe Jackson's 3-D film *Captain Eo*. The movie had been showing since the theme park opened in 1991.

16   Jackson's former maid Blanca Francia alleges that the singer romped and took showers with small boys. She also told lawyers that he 'inappropriately touched' her seven-year-old son.

17   Blanca Francia makes further allegations against Jackson on American TV show 'Hard Copy'. She claims that the star squeezed into a sleeping bag with her son and also gave him money as a gift.

18   Two of Jackson's top aides, lawyer Bert Fields and private eye Anthony Pellicano, mysteriously and suddenly leave his service.

19   It is revealed that one of Jackson's hideouts when he was in Europe getting treatment for his addiction to painkillers was a Tudor-style mansion belonging to businessman Jack Dellal on the Manor Farm estate in Brown Condover, Hampshire.

22   Michael Jackson makes a sensational TV broadcast to plead his innocence. In his emotional speech on cable channel CNN, the star tells how he was humiliated by having to strip completely naked for a police examination.

JANUARY

10   Michael Jackson is snubbed by Britain's music industry after failing to be nominated for any awards at the BRITS, to be held in February.

11   Court papers reveal Jordan Chandler's claims that Jackson would lie on top of him and rub up and down over him, that he taught him to French kiss and had baths with him. Chandler also claims that Jackson masturbated him with both his hand and his mouth.

Jordan Chandler turns fourteen.

18   The deadline set for Jackson to give a legal deposition answering Jordan Chandler's accusations.

21   Michael Jackson agrees to pay Jordan Chandler £30 million after more than a month of secret negotiations. In return Jordan Chandler agrees to drop his civil lawsuit against Jackson.

24   Police say that Jackson was not the victim of a blackmail attempt planned by Evan Chandler and that no charges will be pressed against Jordan's father.

25   Jackson's multi-million-pound settlement with Jordan Chandler is made public.

26   Jackson's lawyer Johnnie Cochrane states:' This agreement is in no way an admission of guilt by Michael Jackson.'

Los Angeles district attorney Gil Garcetti vows

that he will continue the criminal investigation into Jackson despite the settlement.

28   It is revealed that a second boy – not yet named – is being lined up by police to testify against Jackson if child abuse charges are brought against the star.

Jackson is replaced in Pepsi's new £5-million commercial by a chimpanzee.

29   Jackson must see a psychiatrist as a condition of his settlement, reveals Diane Dimond of American TV show 'Hard Copy', stating: 'It was a primary condition for Chandler to settle.'

FEBRUARY

5   Jackson is reported to be launching a lawsuit against LaToya in a bid to stop her revealing sensational new allegations about his sex life.

7   It is reported that a grand jury in Santa Barbara is to hear child abuse evidence against Jackson and then decide whether criminal charges will be brought against the singer.

9   The jury begins hearing testimony. The first witness is Marlon Brando's son Miko, a former employee of Jackson's.

It is revealed that Jackson has applied for a bank loan to help pay his £30-million settlement with Jordan Chandler.

10   Jackson's top female aide Norma Staikos refuses to answer questions about the child abuse allegations for the grand jury.

13   Jackson is offered refuge by an African tribe on the Ivory Coast.

19   Jackson makes his stage comeback at a charity concert called 'The Jackson Family Honours'. It is the first time he has sung on stage in America since the beginning of the scandal.

24   Janet Jackson says she no longer considers her sister

LaToya as part of the family after her constant criticism of Michael.

MARCH

17 Elton John admits that he hid Michael Jackson at his Windsor mansion while he was being treated for addiction to painkillers.

24 Jackson makes his first payment to Jordan Chandler, almost three months after the original settlement. The cheque from the singer's personal account at the City National Bank is for £1.3 million.

30 A second cheque for almost £2 million is put into Jordan Chandler's trust account.

APRIL

2 It is reported that two key witnesses are willing to testify against Jackson. The pair are believed to be a young boy and his mother.

11 Diane Dimond reports on 'Hard Copy' that the police are not going to seek an indictment against Jackson.

12 Denise Pfeiffer from Leicestershire is brought into Beverly Hills Municipal Court where she is accused of harassing Evan Chandler and his family. Pfeiffer is unable to raise $10,000 bail and is remanded in custody. A few days later British actress Lynn Redgrave rescues her by paying her bail.

13 Police probing the case are given more time to produce evidence and sources insist that the investigation will continue for as long as is necessary.

ACKNOWLEDGEMENTS

Many people helped in getting this book together. Among those I would particularly like to single out are Shubana Bhatti and Louise Johncox, who helped me research various sections of the book. Other thanks go to *Daily Mirror* editor David Banks, who let me embark on the project, Don Short my agent, and Val Hudson and Karen Whitlock at my publishers, HarperCollins.

Thanks also to the people who talked frankly and revealingly about Michael Jackson to me – you know who you are.

Hundreds of newspaper and magazine articles and many books and videos about Jackson were also used as sources and references. They include the *Daily Mirror, Sunday Mirror, People, Today, Daily Mail, Mail on Sunday*, London *Evening Standard, The Times, The Sunday Times, Sun, News of the World, Daily Express, Daily Star, Daily Telegraph, Vanity Fair, National Enquirer, Star, New York Post, New York Daily News, Los Angeles Times, Entertainment Weekly* and J. Randy Taraborrelli's biography of Michael Jackson, *The Magic and the Madness*.

I would also like to thank the *Daily Mirror* library staff and its chief on enquiries Derek Drury for all their efforts.

Grateful acknowledgement is made to the following picture agencies for allowing us to reproduce their photographs:

All Action
Alpha
Famous
London Features International Ltd

Sipa Press
Solo Syndication
People in Pictures
Rex Features, London